Triple-Threat
Basketball

Triple-Threat

Basketball

Chuck Mundell

PARKER PUBLISHING COMPANY, INC.

West Nyack, N.Y.

Acknowledgments

I would like to acknowledge the help and training given me by my former coaches, teachers, players, and teammates over the years. I would like to thank my parents, Mr. and Mrs. Emil Mundell, for affording me the opportunity to participate in sports. I would like to acknowledge some of the many coaches that I have had the opportunity to observe and learn from including Norm Cottom, Fred Wampler, Frank Mayfield, George Yaeger and Howard Sharpe—formerly of Terre Haute Gerstmeyer—Glen Curtis, Dave Glascock, Paul Wolf, John Longfellow and Johnny Wooden, all formerly of Indiana State University.

This book is an integration of many ideas concerning ways to play the game of basketball. The Triple Threat concept recognizes that there is more than one way to play the game. I have attempted to mold the best ideas into a system of play which attempts to capitalize upon all of the strong points of the fast break, the control pattern offense, and an aggressive, versatile style of defensive play.

Lastly, I would like to express my deep gratitude to my wife, Norma—Head Coach of our own Triple Threat, Dan, Don, and Debbie—for typing me through graduate and undergraduate degrees at Indiana State University, and many summers of further work at The Ohio State University and The University of California. I am also indebted to her for correcting and typing the manuscript of this book.

What Triple-Threat
Basketball Is and How It
Works

This book is about Triple-Threat Basketball—a system of basketball that has succeeded. This system capitalizes on all of the strong points of the fast break, the control pattern offense, the man-to-man defense, the zone defense, and the pressing defenses, while at the same time it attempts to minimize the weaknesses of each of these.

We call the system the Triple-Threat Attack because it is, just as the name implies, a three pronged, aggressive, relentless attack upon the opposition. It stresses a well-balanced attack through equal emphasis upon the control fast break, the perpetual pattern offense, and upon a strong versatile defensive attack.

This system attempts to make a science out of basketball by playing for the mathematical percentages in all situations. The author believes that it is absurd to stress any one phase of the game of basketball at the expense of another phase. It is possible to be versatile and aggressive and still play full-time basketball. The Triple-Threat team is ready for anything. They cannot be forced to play in an unfamiliar style because they are well versed and familiar with all styles.

This book will show you how to use the control fast break to best advantage. It will demonstrate drills and patterns which will be of value in learning this important weapon. It will show you how to build and develop a perpetual pattern of offensive basketball against a zone or man-to-man defense. Many of these patterns will be illustrated.

It will introduce the "Triple A" defense, a system of aggressive man-to-man, alternating zone, and aggravating press defenses, which are designed to overpower, surprise, and wear down the opposition.

This book will discuss a special type of press defense which has worked well for us against some very tough teams. We call it the Centralia "Red-Dog" double team press. This book will show you how to use what you have to the best advantage and how to develop your team step by step during the playing season, so that your team will be ready and well prepared for the championship tournament.

Chuck Mundell

Table of Contents

Triple-Threat
Basketball

1

The Triple Threat
in Basketball

I believe in full-time basketball. There is no time to rest on the basketball court. The only time to let down or rest is before the game, during time-outs, at half-time, or after the game. Basketball pants have no pockets; the benches are on the sideline. A basketball player who only plays offense or only plays defense is really just half of a basketball player.

A player must be in top physical and mental condition in order to give his best at all times. Playing basketball is not a part-time job. A point scored or prevented in the first minute of the game may turn out to be the winning point. It is difficult to learn to play with this aggressive attitude—but it is a must in Triple-Threat Basketball.

What is the triple threat?

Triple-Threat Basketball is, as its name implies, a three-pronged, aggressive, continuous attack upon the opposition. When you have the ball, think about beating the other team to your goal. If you don't get a really good shot, work your plays or patterns until you do get the good percentage shot. If you don't have the ball, think about getting it back! In other words the Triple-Threat team should:

1. Always be a threat to fast break.
2. When you don't get the advantage on the fast break, keep the ball until you do get the most favorable shot, with a controlled, pressure offense.
3. Work as hard on defense as you do on offense.

The fast break and the control offense are very important parts of basketball, but defense is just as important. Be aggressive at all times on defense, and be able to use as many different defensive attacks as you do offensive. Defense is half of the ball game—it should be treated as such!

Formula for success

This idea of basketball play may be expressed by the formula: Control Offense + Fast Break + Aggressive Defense = Victory.
$$(\text{CO} + \text{FB} + \text{AD} = \text{V})$$
The ingredients need to be refined through fundamentals and the catalyst for this formula is desire.

You play both offense and defense

Teams which claim a good defensive average are often just low-scoring teams. They play Keepaway and use up time, often letting good shots go and finally taking the bad ones. On the other hand, teams with high scoring averages are often hustlers in the offensive game but merely spectators on the defensive end of the court. I believe that a basketball team should have a strong, aggressive offense and be tough on defense at the same time.

Different styles of play

There are basically four different kinds of basketball teams. The style of play sometimes varies with locality. These styles can be described as:

1. The defensive-minded teams
2. The fast-break-minded teams
3. The ball-control teams
4. The control-fast-break teams

The defensive teams

Although there is much to be said for a hard-working, aggressive, defensive-minded team, such a team often concentrates on defense at the expense of a well-organized offense. They often play extreme ball-control along with their hustling defense. The idea sometimes seems to be that if the other team does not have the ball, they can't be scoring with it.

Most defensive-minded teams seem to come to life only when the other team gets the ball. They do not take full advantage of their offensive scoring opportunities.

The fast-break-minded teams

Many teams have been successful with a well-organized, aggressive fast-break style of attack. It is a weapon which is employed today by many great basketball teams in the United States.

With the fast-break-minded teams, the name of the game is "Run!" They often let down on the defensive end of the floor. They like to run and shoot. They quite often play a sloppy brand of basketball. If you are not careful, you start playing their type of game, and eventually play into their hands. This team always looks for the fast break and often takes the low percentage shot or the forced shot. They even encourage you to shoot, so that they can get their hands on the ball and come back to life. The running team is often very tough when they are hitting well and their ball-handling is sharp. They are in trouble on off nights, when their shooting percentage drops or their ball-handling gets too careless.

The ball-control teams

Fast-break people and ball-control people are very often at odds as to how the game of basketball should be played. The ball-control people swear *by* their patient, well-organized style of play and the fast-break people swear *at* it. A style of play where you can control the way that the game is being played on the floor has its merits, and many coaches have been very successful with this style of play.

The ball-control teams figure that if they can control the ball 55 or 65 per cent of the time and take only the high percentage shots, they can win the ball game. Often the ball-control teams are falsely given credit for being great defensive teams because of the low scores of their ball games. They usually have a well-organized pattern of attack, running their plays and patterns methodically until they get the shot that they are looking for. They sometimes rock you to sleep on defense and then take advantage of your defensive error. Some of the disadvantages of the ball-control style are that it is very hard to teach and takes hours of working on offensive patterns, often at the expense of time which should be spent on defense. Another drawback is that a few ball-handling errors can be very costly to this offensive strategy. Ball-control teams must know each other very well and must be careful in their judgement of when they have a good percentage shot. They are in trouble if they get very far behind in the score. They are at their best when they can control the lead in the score.

The control-fast-break teams

The control-fast-break offense can vary its attack from time to time within a game, or against certain opponents. More and more teams seem to be moving toward this middle-of-the-road type of offense. Basketball, like politics, seems to have left-wingers, right-wingers, liberals, and conservatives.

The control-fast-break teams look for fast-break opportunities, but they will pass up the forced shot or the low percentage shot in favor of a more controlled offensive pattern. If their fast-break attack fails to produce an outnumbered situation or a high percentage shot, they will bring the ball back out court and start an organized offensive pattern. They do not just run and shoot. They try to work a compromise between the fast-break and the ball-control styles of play. They attempt to draw the advantages and eliminate some of the disadvantages from each style of play.

The control-fast-break is often very hard to teach, and it leaves a lot of decisions on the shoulders of the players. It is very easy to start to play run and shoot and then to get too careless. It is also very easy to lose your daring and start to play too cautious a game.

The philosophy of the Triple-Threat attack

In Triple-Threat Basketball we attempt to utilize all the advantages and eliminate all the disadvantages of each style of play. This may sound very idealistic and impossible to accomplish, but each of the other styles of play mentioned has its own elements of idealism. Someone once said, "The game of basketball is a series of mistakes, and the team that makes the fewest mistakes eventually wins the game."

Triple-Threat Basketball is full-time basketball, with emphasis being placed on all phases of the game, and not just on some particular part of it. The style may vary with the opponent's style of play, to force the opposition to play in an unfamiliar style.

The Triple-Threat team is ready for anything. They cannot be forced to play in an unfamiliar style, because they are familiar with all styles. The secret of the Triple-Threat attack is found in the Boy Scout motto: *Be Prepared.*

The Triple Threat is a well-integrated attack which utilizes the best and strongest points of the four basic styles of play used in basketball. It is very hard to teach, and like anything else worthwhile it takes time and very hard work. This integrated style of play must be developed day by day. Every practice session should be well-planned and have a definite purpose. If there is no learning—there is no teaching.

The Triple-Threat style of play is a very challenging way to play the game of basketball. Much of its success depends upon the ability of the individual player to make the right decisions at the right time. This comes from proper instruction and experience. The coach who asks that his players try to give their best at all times should be prepared to give in like measure. He owes this much to his players.

Create happenings

Like modern art, the art of basketball must create happenings. To the casual observer many opportunities on the basketball court just seem to happen. Players just seem to be in the right place at the right time. Triple-Threat Basketball attempts to create these happenings. Offense and defense cannot be left to luck—they must be well-planned and thoroughly practiced. Luck is really to be found at the intersection of preparedness and opportunity.

2

Developing an Aggressive, Versatile Championship Team

All coaches work toward the development of a championship team. The poor coach cries, "I have no material"—the good coach says, "I'll do the best I can with what I have."

The attitude of the coach is of utmost importance in the development of the team. If the coach is visibly disappointed with his prospects for the coming year, his attitude will rub off on his players and greatly hinder his chances of improving their individual or team efforts. The coach must always be optimistic in his approach. He must make his players believe in themselves. The good coach must be a good salesman. He must sell the team on his ability as a coach. He must sell his ideas and styles of play. He must sell the importance of individual fundamentals, of team play, of the proper attitude, of physical conditioning, of good offensive and defensive patterns.

It is very important that a coach develop his individual philosophy concerning the game—it is more important that he learn to put his philosophy into practice. Words and ideas are only tools which must be used with skill to develop a quality product—a championship team.

Learning to walk before you can run

It would be ridiculous to start to build a house without first laying a solid foundation. It would be worthless to try to teach a first-grader the entire theory of relativity.

It is just as ridiculous to try to develop a fast-break team without good ball-handling fundamentals, or to try to use new patterns or styles if your team is not ready to absorb them. A good coach plans his play and then plays his plan. The over-all plan should develop slowly and be built up bit by bit.

Don't try to use last year's plans this year. Every season and every ball game is a new one. Appropriate new plans must be developed and employed. The development of a championship team must be organized to continue over the entire season. Lessons learned early in the season may set the foundation for victory later.

Importance of fundamentals

All good coaches are believers in the importance of individual fundamentals. To try to build a championship basketball team without emphasis on individual fundamentals such as proper foot-work, shooting, defensive stance, dribbling, passing, offensive maneuvers, rebounding, cutting, screening, pivoting, defensive switching, and sliding through would be absurd. Good individual fundamentals are the backbone of any championship basketball team. The coach must sell his players on the importance of these little things. Someone once said, "If you take care of the little things in life, the big things will take care of themselves." This is also true in basketball. Many great plans have fallen through and many potential victories been lost because of little things. Good individual fundamentals can make an average team into a championship team. Sloppy fundamentals can make a potential champion into an also-ran.

Built-in fundamentals

It is not enough to say to your players, "Men—you must have good fundamentals." The coach must be a good teacher. He must devise ways and learning situations in which good fundamentals will be acquired.

There are many fundamentals drills which are very good to use in early season practice, but you must be careful that you don't over-use them. When the coach says "drill" many boys will automatically let down or say, "Ah-h-h, do we *have* to?"

We try to put some "Fun" into the "fun-damentals" with our "built-in" fundamentals. We don't use the same drills day after day. We change the drills, combine them into new ones or make games or competitive situations out of them.

For example, you can stress good fundamentals while you are running your offensive patterns or plays. Make sure that your boys use good footwork, make sharp passes, set screens properly, use correct form in the dribble, make proper cuts, etc. Do not allow laxness or sloppiness in fundamentals. The old saying "practice makes perfect" is not always correct—it does no good to practice the improper form. In fact, it is disastrous to practice techniques over and over again sloppily. Only *right* practice makes perfect.

When the players seem to tire, think of ways to make drills competitive. For example, on our rebound drill we may set up five on five. One group is the offensive team and the other defensive. The coach or manager shoots the ball from out court and the defensive team practices blocking out and getting the rebound. The team that gets the rebound gets one point. The teams change from defense to offense in positioning. The team that scores ten points first wins. The winning team is then challenged by a new group, while the losers run a given number of laps around the gym floor (Diagram 2-1).

Fast-break and defensive drills can be made competitive be-

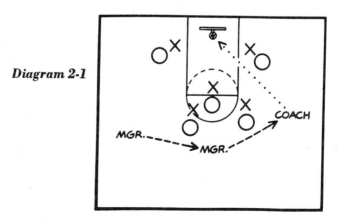

Diagram 2-1

tween teams or on an individual basis. Sloppy fundamentals should not be tolerated during scrimmage or at any other time. Play should be stopped and any errors corrected immediately.

There are many ways in which fundamentals can be built in. They can be taught along with conditioning drills and offensive and defensive play. Most players prefer to run with a purpose in mind rather than just around the track or gym for physical conditioning. Fast-break drills, for example, can be devised to serve other purposes such as physical conditioning, ball handling at top speed, timing, getting the rebound, getting back on defense, faking, dribbling, pivoting, etc.

Build on a solid foundation

Fundamentals are the foundation of a good basketball team. If you don't have a large foundation, don't try to build a tall building. If you expect to build tall, first increase the size of the foundation.

Many young coaches make the mistake of trying to do too much too soon. They waste their time trying to develop new plays or patterns when the players are not executing the old plays in the proper manner. They are so eager to teach new styles and ideas that they never fully develop any of them. The players become confused and the fundamentals foundation starts to crumble. This is sometimes referred to as over-coaching.

The coach must be careful not to try to develop too fast. His team should grow throughout the year, but he should not force their growth when they are not yet ready to tackle something new. Each phase of the game should be developed, and new things should be added only if the old have been fully learned.

Be versatile

The versatile team is the hardest team to beat. If a team can play well using a certain style of play, they can have a very good team, but if a team can play well using many styles, they can be champions! There are many ways to play the game of basketball; most of them are basically sound and have certain advantages and disadvantages.

Developing the "add-on" offense and defense

We like to have open-end offensive patterns and defensive plans upon which we can build continually during the season.

How far we can go depends upon the ability of the individual players to grow and develop in their individual skill and knowledge of the game. We usually start with a simple basic man-to-man offense and a man-to-man defense. When the team fully understands and can use these, we start to build and add on new plays and new dimensions in defense. By the end of the season (tournament time) we are quite versatile. We are ready to cope with many more situations than we were able to at the start of the season.

Continuity is maintained by basic rules and fundamentals which must be followed on each of the man-to-man offenses, the zone offensive patterns, the man-to-man defense, and the zone defense. These rules are followed for each new strategy which is added on to the basic options and patterns of play (see chapters 8 and 11).

Work toward a goal—the championship

Few—if any—basketball teams "luck" themselves into the championship. It comes about through a lot of very hard work, planning, sacrifice, and good teaching, combined with a winning attitude. To the casual observer or fan, it appears that the team may have gotten quite lucky at the end of the season. But this is the time of year when basic planning and early season work pays dividends. Some teams hope to *get* the breaks, but the championship team *makes its own* breaks.

Organization is very important in aiming toward the championship. The coach must know what he is trying to accomplish and must make himself understood at all times. He must organize practice sessions, games, trips, schedules, equipment, training program, and himself very carefully. He must know what is going to happen almost before it occurs. A coach does not need a crystal ball, but he should be so well-organized that other people are convinced that he has one.

A coach must be very careful in the selection of his player material. Consider the whole player—not just his offensive or shooting capabilities. Consider also such things as defensive ability, team play, desire, physical condition, and potential for improvement. Ask such questions as: Has he reached his peak? Is he still developing and growing in ability? What does the team lack? Could this boy contribute to the team? Could he fulfill a basic need of the team? Look farther into the season than just the first game.

In all probability the team that wins the championship planned to do so all along. They may have surprised other people, and perhaps even themselves; but they must have laid the plans for their conquest early in the season or in previous years of work.

A championship team must have confidence that they are prepared to carry home the big trophy. The players must have confidence in their ability, their coach, in each other, and in their strategy for victory. They must feel that the plans were really their own ideas. If they feel that they are in on the planning, they really want the plan to work, and wanting to is a good part of the battle. A championship team must set their goals a little higher than they really think that they are capable of reaching—they may surprise themselves!

3

The Control-Fast Break

The control-fast break is a
basketball strategy designed to gain an advantage on the opposition by getting men in the scoring area before they can organize
their defense. The control-fast break attempts to gain this advantage without unnecessarily risking loss of the ball. If the attempt
fails it is possible to make a smooth transition into a controlled
pressure type of offense.

The threat of the fast break

The control-fast break is a well-organized plan of attack
which is an ever-present threat to the opposition. The fact that
you hold this threat over their heads gives you an edge over the
opponent to start with. It gives them one more thing to worry
about and tends to weaken their defensive and offensive potential. If they do not attempt to defense your fast-break threat, you
can make believers out of them by cashing in on their defensive
weakness. If they do attempt to defense your fast-break attack, it
will give you an opportunity to get better shots from your regular
patterns.

The threat of the fast break can make the other team nervous when they are trying to run their offensive plan of attack. If they put too many men in the scoring area, you can push the fast break and capitalize on this defensive weakness. If they don't, this will confuse their regular plays and patterns.

Fast-break threat helps you control the boards

The fast-break threat also gives your team a much better opportunity to control your defensive backboard. The opposition must be ready to drop back on defense as soon as they attempt a shot at the goal. This gives your team the opportunity to move in and control the rebound without so much pressure or contention on the boards.

Controlling the pace of the game

The control-fast break team can more or less control the pace of the game by speeding up or slowing down their offensive attack. The strict ball-control teams are in trouble when they are forced to play a fast game because they are behind in the score. They have to play an unfamiliar game, and they play into the hands of the opponent.

The strictly run-and-shoot teams have problems if they are forced to play a slow, deliberate type of game. They may start to give up good shots in order to get their hands on the ball again, and if they fail to score it may start a vicious circle of events which can lead to their downfall.

Ready for anything

The control-fast break team is well prepared and ready for any eventuality. They are constantly putting offensive pressure on the opposition. They are in a very good position to force the other team to play in an unfamiliar manner, and they are ready to play in any style, if it is necessary for them to do so.

The control-fast break should be an integral part of your total plan for victory

The fast break is only a part of the three-pronged attack of Triple Threat Basketball. It should be a sharp, well-organized plan; but you should not concentrate on this phase of the game at the expense of the regular offensive pattern, nor at the expense of team or individual effort on defense. Too many fast-break teams make the mistake of over-specialization.

The cardinal principles of the control-fast break

1. *Be a fast-break threat at all times.* Don't walk down the basketball court if you can run. Be alert and look for all fast-break opportunities. If you are in control of the ball you can always hold up if it is necessary to do so. It does not cost anything to try! It takes effort and energy to run, and your boys must be in top physical and mental condition to make full use of this threat.

2. *Outnumber the opposition with the fast break.* Try to get men in your scoring area before they can get their men back on defense. Get there first with the most. This idea is especially important against zone defense teams which use the principle of team effort or assigned areas of defensive play. Try to outrun them down the court.

3. *Get the rebound and pass the ball out at the earliest opportunity.* You can't attempt a fast break unless you first get the ball. Rebounding is an important part of defense and of the control-fast break. The first pass out of traffic after the rebound is the most important. This quick pass out may determine whether you get your fast-break attempt. Many players have the very bad habit of trying to dribble the ball out of traffic after a rebound. They often get into trouble with this practice, and even if they are successful in dribbling to the side they give the opposing team plenty of time for the offense-to-defense transition. The fast break may be started by several different kinds of passes. The two-hand overhead pass is one of the best passes to use for the quick outlet pass. The rebounder keeps the ball up high, turns, and looks for the pass receiver. This type of pass not only saves time, but also helps to prevent the steal or double team situation.

4. *Pass the ball—don't dribble.* Never dribble the ball if you can pass it up the basketball court. Dribbling should be a safety valve to be used only when absolutely necessary. The dribble slows down the fast-break attempt. The fastest man cannot outrun a good, snappy pass. (We often demonstrate this important idea by lining up four players along the side of the basketball court. The fastest man on the squad tries to dribble from one end of the court to the other, while the other four men pass another ball from end to end. The passed ball is usually down at the other end with four snappy passes long before the dribbler is at half-court.) Look up the court and if there is a man open ahead of you pass the ball to him.

5. *Shoot the ball on the fast-break attempt only if you get a good shot.* Take the shot at the end of the fast break only if it is a high percentage shot. Don't waste the efforts of four other men by an off-balance or "hope" shot. We like to shoot only when we think that we have better than a 50-50 chance of scoring. (Our teams have scored an average of 48 per cent of their field goal attempts in games during the past four years.)

6. *Appreciate possession of the ball.* Don't give up the basketball without first getting a good attempt at scoring. Don't take foolish chances. If you have to, stop the fast break and throw the ball back out to a guard or trailer. Set up patterns or plays from which you can get good percentage shots if your fast-break attempt fails. Have sharp ball-handling fundamentals. Know your capabilities and limitations. Play for the percentages, but don't be overly cautious. You must learn to take advantage of each situation as it presents itself.

7. *Don't give up too easily on the fast-break attempt.* You must keep up the fast-break attempt all during the game. Don't give up. Make the opposition worry about defensing your fast break all during the game. If you let up here, they can concentrate their defense in other areas. Even if you cash in on the fast break only once or twice during the game, your running is not wasted. There are other advantages to the running attempt, such as keeping their offense off balance, getting defensive rebounds, and occupying their defense. The one time that you score may be the winning bucket. The fast break is a good weapon: use it wisely, well, and often.

Basic rebound pattern

On all defensive rebounds we send three men inside to form the rebound triangle (1, 2, and 3) and our other two men (4 and 5) play the high rebounders (Diagram 3-1). This pattern leads very simply into our two basic fast-break patterns.

The three-lane attack

In the three-lane attack, as soon as we get the rebound the men playing the high bounders (4 and 5) break to the side to receive the first pass out. If 1 gets the rebound, 2 will break to that sideline as a safety. If we can't pass to 4 or 5, then we pass to 2. As soon as 3 sees that 1 has the rebound he breaks down the

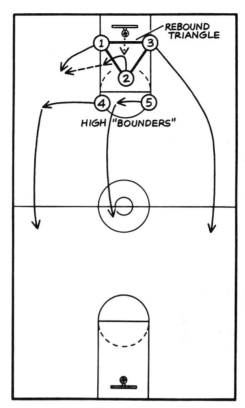

Diagram 3-1

outside lane. Players 3, 4, and 5 fill the lanes and pass the ball back and forth as they go at full speed toward the other basket (Diagram 3-2). Players 1 and 2 will come in a little later as the trailers (Diagram 3-3).

If the ball comes off the other side, 3 gets the rebound, 2 is the safety pass man, and 1 will fill the outside lane (Diagram 3-4).

If the ball comes off to middle man 2, then the inside man that 2 is facing, either 1 or 3, will become the safety man, and the other will fill the third lane.

The four-lane pattern

If we have difficulty starting the three-lane fast break or passing the ball to our safety man, then we start the four-lane pattern. The idea here is that the other team will have more time to mass their defense and we may have to settle for a four-on-three or five-on-four situation, instead of the two-on-one or three-on-two. In the four-lane attack we pass to safety man 2 on the

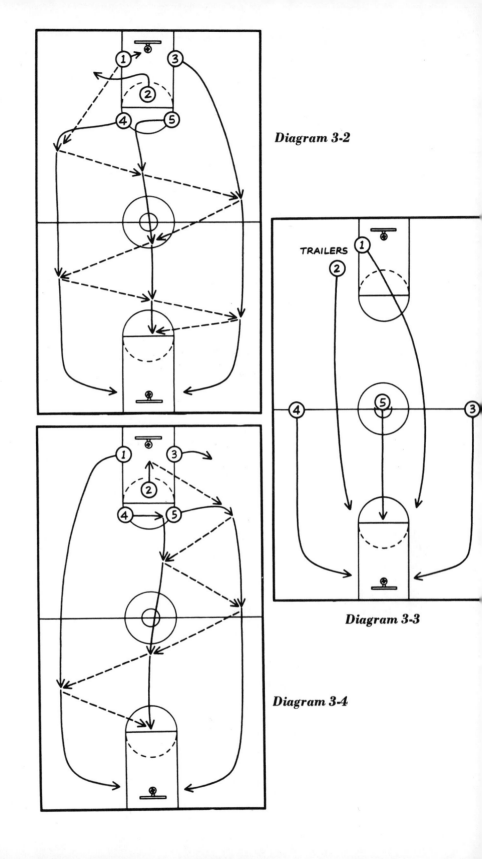

Diagram 3-2

Diagram 3-3

Diagram 3-4

TRAILERS

side, while 1, who got the rebound, will fill one of the middle lanes. Player 2 will pass up to 4 or 5 or back to 1. We then move on down, passing the ball back and forth in the four-lane attack. Player 2 will come in as a trailer (Diagram 3-5).

If the rebound comes off to 3, then 2 will be the safety man on that side, and 3 will pass to 2 and then fill one of the middle lanes. Player 2 will pass to 4 or 5, or back to 3 and then come in as a trailer (Diagram 3-6).

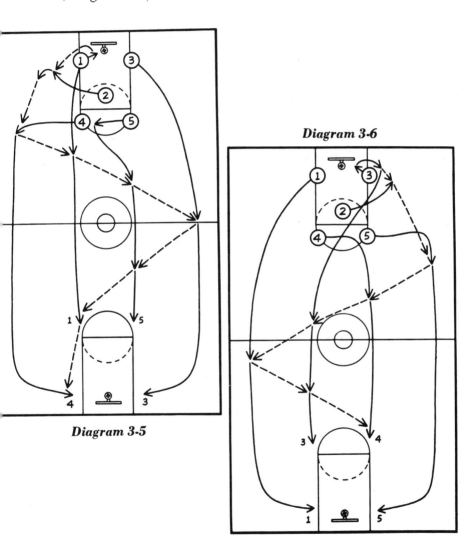

Diagram 3-6

Diagram 3-5

If the rebound goes to 2, then the man that he faces, either 1 or 3, will break for the safety pass. Player 2 will pass to 1 or 3 and then fill one of the middle lanes. Player 1 or 3 will then pass to 4 or 5 or back to 2 and then come in as a trailer (Diagram 3-7).

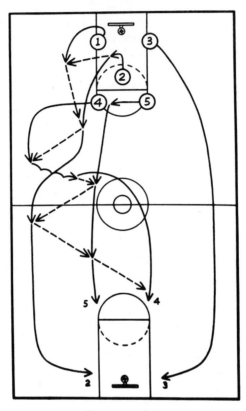

Diagram 3-7

4

How to Use the Control-

Fast Break

The chief difference between the run-and-shoot fast break and the control-fast break is in the use and application of the fast-break fundamentals. The run-and-shoot fast-break teams have to fast break; with the control-fast-break-team, this is just one of their weapons.

The run-and-shoot team is not happy if they are not running. The control-fast-break-team can adjust to a slower pace and still keep up the fast-break threat while exploring other avenues to victory.

The use of the control-fast break is difficult to teach. When to fast-break and when not to, when to push the fast break and when to set it up—these are hard decisions for individual players to make.

This knowledge comes through hours of practice, drill, instruction, and personal experience. Through proper guidance this should be another part of your team play which should constantly improve during the playing season. This craftmanship will come through co-operation, team play, personal sacrifice, and patience.

Fast-break starting points

We attempt the fast break from all possible starting points. We are always ready to run. This constant threat keeps the opponent anxious on offense and worried about getting back on defense. This is a great psychological advantage at the very start. We can attempt the fast break in several situations: defensive rebound, controlled tip, against a full-court press, on a scored goal.

DEFENSIVE REBOUNDS

This is one of the best times to start a fast-break attempt. Each time that we get a defensive rebound we think about the fast-break attempt. We attempt the fast break until there is no longer any hope of getting an offensive advantage or a good percentage shot. The quick pass out from the basket traffic is the key to the success of the fast break. If we can not get the pass out fast, then we try a delayed fast break or else slow down for a pattern offense. To get the rebound, each player must turn his back to his opponent and block him out from the inside rebounding position. We attempt to move in with a rebounding triangle, composed of the pivot man and the two forwards. Our guards move into the circle to play the high bouncing rebounds (Diagram 4-1). We sometimes rebound by use of the cross block. The three inside men move in front of their opposite men. We use this if our opponent's inside men are getting around us, and we use it especially on the offensive board where we may be blocked out (Diagram 4-2).

Diagram 4-1	*Diagram 4-2*
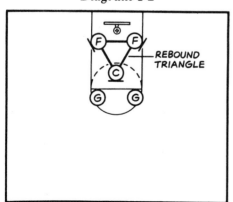	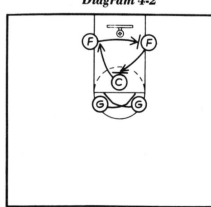

CONTROLLED TIP

If we feel that there is a better than fifty per cent chance that we can control a jump ball (at mid-court or in the defensive court), we may line up with the two forwards on the offensive side of the circle and our two guards on the defensive side. (If a guard or forward is jumping, the center will replace him in one of these positions.) We start the move by having G-1, the guard who is in back of our tipper, break around to the side we intend to tip to. This guard starts his move just as the ball goes up from the official's hand. The forward, F-1 (we do not intend to tip to him), is sent back into G-1's position as a safety, to steal or help on defense in the event we do not control the tip. The other guard, G-2, is ready to drop back on defense as soon as G-1 goes around him. We try to tip the ball to F-2 if possible. If he is covered we may tip long to G-1, who is on the move. If either of these tips is successful, we are on the move toward a fast-break attempt. We fill the three lanes and go on our fast break.

Diagram 4-3

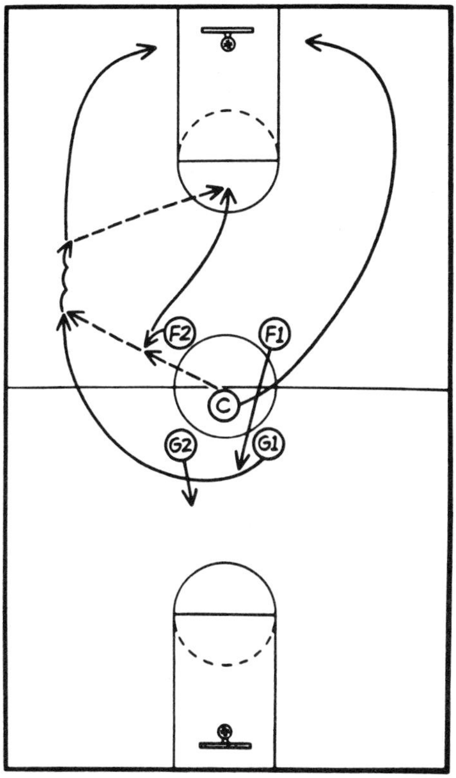

G-1 will fill the left lane, F-2 will be the middle man, and C will take the right hand lane after the tip. If for some reason F-2 could not get into the center lane soon enough, C would take it, and F-1 would try to take the right hand lane. F-1 and G-2 normally would come in as trailers if we did not score on the three lane fast break (Diagram 4-3).

AGAINST A FULL-COURT PRESS

Against a full-court press, we try to get the ball to mid-court fast and outnumber the back court men before the down-court pressers can get back on defense. (This is the principle of being able to pass the ball faster than a defensive man can run.) On a scored basket by the other team our forwards break for the center line on each side. (We use the guards in some situations.) The pivot man breaks for the center of the floor (Diagram 4-4). One guard, G-1, takes the ball out quickly and the other guard, G-2, breaks to meet the ball. If we get the ball in to G-2, he looks to pass the ball up to one of the forwards or the pivot man, who may have to reverse and break to meet the pass (Diagram 4-5).

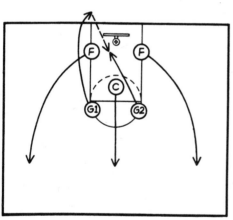

Diagram 4-4

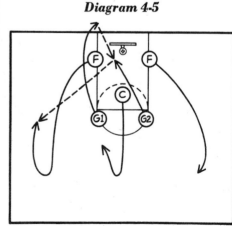

Diagram 4-5

If G-2 can't pass up court, then he passes to G-1, who breaks in court from out of bounds, who will in turn look for a pass up court. (Diagram 4-6).

If we can't get the ball in to G-2, then F-1 and F-2 will reverse and break toward the ball to get the ball in bounds. F-1 or F-2 will then look up court and try to pass the ball to the pivot man to start the three-lane fast break (Diagram 4-7).

If we can't get the ball in to G-2, F-1, or F-2, then the pivot man will reverse toward the defensive foul line and the forwards will again reverse toward the middle line. We must get the ball in to one of them. If we hit the pivot man, he passes up court to F-1 or F-2, and we are on our way to a three-lane fast break (Diagram 4-8).

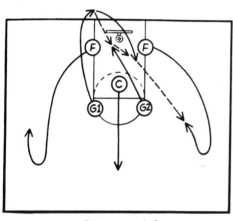

Diagram 4-6

Diagram 4-7

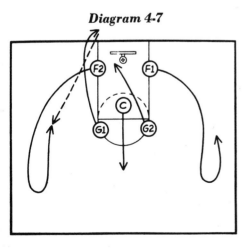

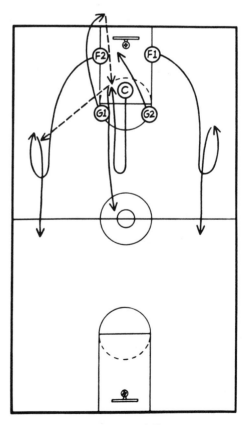

Diagram 4-8

This may sound like a lot to accomplish in under five seconds, but it really isn't too hard to perfect if each man knows his job and does it. The most important thing to remember against a press defense is not to get excited. Keep your head and work your plan.

SCORED GOAL

Often on a scored goal by the opponent we will have an inside man grab the ball out of the net and step out of bounds for a quick throw in. We may use this on a field goal or after a scored free throw. The man who gets the ball may step out, pivot, and fire a hook pass or a baseball pass to a man breaking toward the ball or to a side-court spot (Diagrams 4-9, 4-10, 4-11).

As soon as we get the ball, we start our three-lane fast break, with the two back men coming in as trailers. We may try this more often against a zone defense, because the zone bases much of its effectiveness on a set, well-organized defensive stance.

Diagram 4-9   *Diagram 4-10*

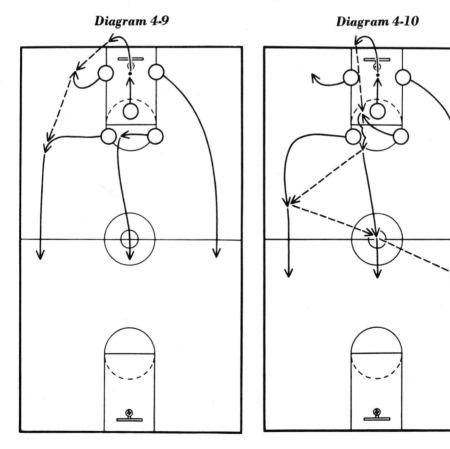

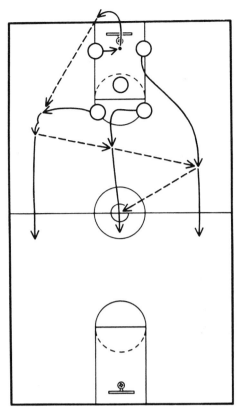

Diagram 4·11

Rules of the fast break

In order for the fast-break attack to be successful there are several basic rules that each player must constantly keep in mind. Without teamwork, timing, and thinking—we call this our "T" formation—the fast break cannot result in a scored field goal.

1. *Think fast break.* Each time we get a hold on the ball, we think about outrunning the other team in order to get them outnumbered. (You only need to catch one of their five men asleep in order to get an advantage.)

2. *Always keep spread.* Do not bunch up. It only helps their defense concentrate their strength and you get in each other's way. If two offensive men come in toward the basket close together, then it only takes one good defensive man to cover both of them. If you are spread, one man can't possibly cover both men at one time.

3. *Cut the corners square.* When coming down court do not round off the corners. Cut them square, about six to ten feet from the base line and three feet from the sideline. If the outside man is too close to the center man, or rounds the corners, he is not in good position to receive the pass for a possible lay-up or short jumper. One defensive man can also have time to move from one man to another (Diagrams 4-12, 4-13).

Cut the corners square and go wide along the side line.

4. *Stop at the foul line.* On the three-on-two, if the ball ends up with the center man, he should stop before he gets to the foul line and make the defensive men commit themselves (either drop back or come forward to cover the man with the ball). If the defense hangs back, then the center man takes a good jump shot from the foul line. You can't get a better shot than this on any offense (Diagram 4-14).

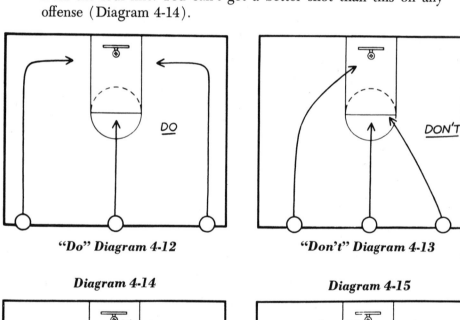

"Do" Diagram 4-12   *"Don't" Diagram 4-13*

Diagram 4-14   *Diagram 4-15*

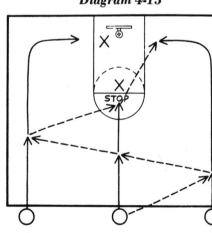

If the defense sends a man out to cover the center man, then he fakes and feeds the ball off to the man coming in on either side, who should be open under the basket (Diagram 4-15).

5. *Stop along the base line.* If we should end up with the ball on the side, instead of in the middle (which we usually prefer), we use the same commit principle. The side man with the ball stops six to eight feet from the basket along the base line and makes the defense commit themselves (Diagram 4-16). He can then either shoot a short jumper or feed off to the center man or bounce-pass to the other end man (Diagram 4-17).

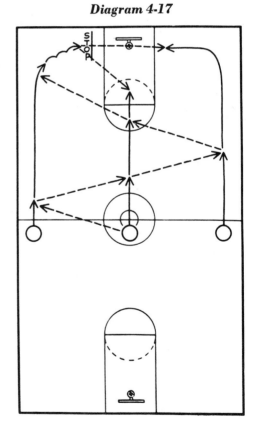

Diagram 4-17

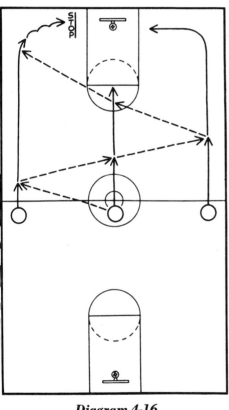

Diagram 4-16

6. *Always go as a team.* It takes a lot of teamwork to run the fast break. One man cannot do it by himself. When you get the ball, yell "go". All the players should start from their positions and move to fill the lanes for the fast-break pattern. The fast break does not work if the players break one at a time. You must run in a great wave and have perfect timing to get the advantage that you are seeking by the quick attack.

7. *Take the ball with you.* Don't start the fast break too soon. First make sure that your team has possession of the ball. Break into your spots to start the fast break, and when your team gets their hands on the ball get it out quickly and start the fast-break attempt. Take the ball with you and go as a group. The exception to this is when we may send down a sleeper or give one man permission to break down court with the shot. We will try this if we are controlling the backboards very well, or if the other team is taking too much of an offensive gamble by sending in all of their men on the boards. A few quick passes down court will force their defense to mobilize sooner and give us more room to get the rebound.

8. *Put the fast into it.* The fast break means just that—fast. You can not run a slow, set, deliberate pattern, telegraphing your positions and plays, and expect to have the fast break successful. You must outrun the opposition to the other end of the floor. Quickness and teamwork are just as important to the success of the fast break as speed. Quickness means reacting rapidly in a positive manner to fast-break opportunities and moving into the proper floor position. You must learn to think fast in order to act fast.

5

Cashing In on the
Fast Break

The fast break is a weapon which
is used in varying degrees by most basketball teams today. It
may be a great asset or it may turn into a liability, depending
upon how it is used and whether it is developed into an integral
part of the total offensive plan. A basketball team with poor
offensive fundamentals is just as apt to be a failure with the fast
break as with any other style of play. Reckless chances, careless
or telegraphed passes, and forced or off-balance shots cannot be
tolerated. A team must learn early their capabilities and limitations.

Fast-break situations

The chief principle of the fast break is to take quick advantage
of the opponent, obtaining a very favorable shot at the basket.
There are several fast-break situations which may develop during
any game.

ONE-ON-NONE

This we expect to happen infrequently during the game, but we are on the alert to take advantage of it as soon as possible. We break fast on an intercepted or deflected pass. On occasion we may send a guard down as a sleeper and try to hit him with a baseball pass. We try this especially if we are controlling the boards well, or the other team is zoning or is a little slow in the transition from offense to defense.

TWO-ON-ONE

We may get the two-on-one situation on an intercepted pass, a steal, a loose ball, or a high bounding rebound. Occasionally we catch the opposition napping after a travel or lane violation, after the official has given us the ball. Our two men spread out on the floor and try to get the defensive man to commit himself to one of them (Diagram 5-1). We would like to favor one side of the floor in a situation similar to our three-lane fast break, except that the

Diagram 5-1	*Diagram 5-2*

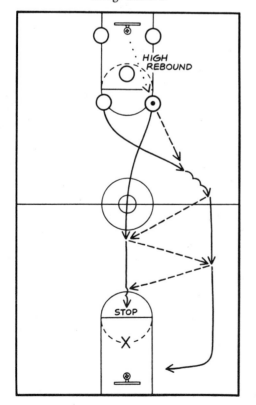
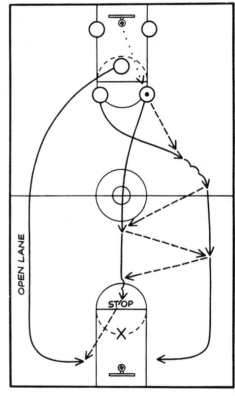

outside lane is still open for another man to come in for a possible easy score (Diagram 5-2).

THREE-ON-TWO

We usually get this situation after a defensive rebound (field goal or free throw) or from the quick pass in bounds after a scored bucket. We spread the defense by having the man with the ball end up on or near the free-throw line. The other two men come in from each side, near the base line. On the three-on-two situation, one of the defensive men must commit himself and cover the man with the ball. If he doesn't, then the man at the free-throw line shoots a jump shot. This is as good a shot as you can get with any offense, and you have two men coming in on the boards for a possible rebound. If one defensive man moves out to cover the man with the ball, then we fire the ball to whichever of the two baseline men is open (Diagram 5-3).

If we happen to end up with the ball on the side, we use the same commit principle. The side man stops eight to ten feet from

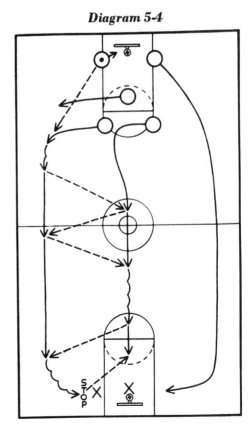

Diagram 5-3   **Diagram 5-4**

the basket and makes the defense commit himself. The man with
the ball can shoot, feed off to the other baseline man, the foul line
player, or to a trailer, or come around a screen set by the center
man or the trailer (Diagram 5-4).

FOUR-ON-THREE

This is a four-lane pattern which we may attempt after a slow
or delayed pass out of a rebound. Two men will split the center
lanes and two will go in the outside lanes. We cross in the back-
court, going behind the man we pass to. In the offensive court,
after we cross the center line, we line up in four lanes and try to
get the four-on-three situation. (Diagram 5-5).

We try to end up with the ball at the foul line on either side of
the circle. We feel that we can do more with the ball here than on
the side (Diagram 5-6).

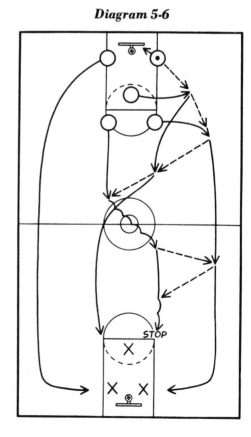

Diagram 5-6

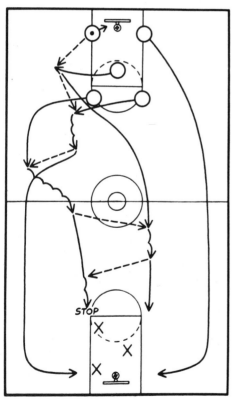

Diagram 5-5

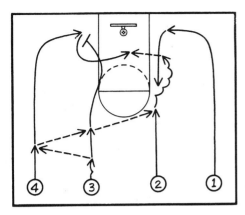

Diagram 5-7

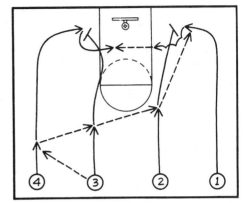

Diagram 5-8

If we can't feed off to an open man or get a good jump shot, we use moving screens to try to get open. Player 1 cuts back to screen for 2, who dribbles around a moving screen set by 1. Player 3 may then go down and screen for 4, who may come around for a pass from 2 under the goal. Player 2 has the option to drive, shoot a jumper, or feed to 4 (Diagram 5-7).

If we happen to end up with the ball on the base line, we have the man who made the last pass (Player 2), set a screen for 1 to drive around. At the same time, 3 sets a screen for 4. Player 1 can get a jump shot in the key or else feed off to 4 coming around the screen (Diagram 5-8).

FIVE-ON-FOUR

The five-on-four situation may come about with the use of the trailers. We continue to push the fast break, even if all of the men in our three-lane pattern are covered tightly. One trailer comes in on each side of the circle. We hope to have one of our trailers open for a jumper, if four or fewer of the opponent's defensive men are back at this time (Diagram 5-9).

The trailers can also become screeners. Player 4 may screen for 2 or 1, and 5 may screen for 3 (Diagram 5-10).

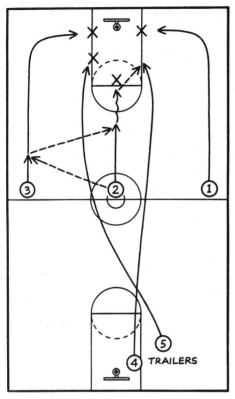

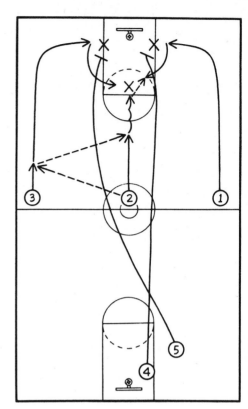

Diagram 5-9   Diagram 5-10

Converting a two-on-two into a three-on-two

If our two-on-one situation is covered and a two-on-two situation exists, we try to move on into a three-on-two by the quick appearance of the third man in the empty lane. This is why we prefer to run our two-on-one down one side of the floor (Diagram 5-11).

Converting a three-on-three into a four-on-three

If our three-lane fast break is well covered, one of our trailers moves in to break for the basket (Diagram 5-12). Or stops to set a post for the man with the ball to drive around (Diagram 5-13).

Using the trailers

The trailers, 4 and 5, may hang back a little and break into the act when they see the time to do so. They may try to break

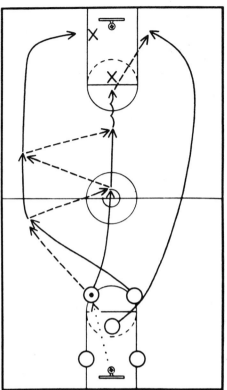

Diagram 5-11

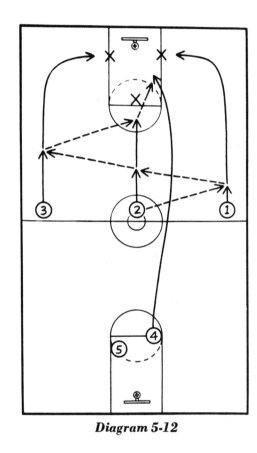

Diagram 5-12

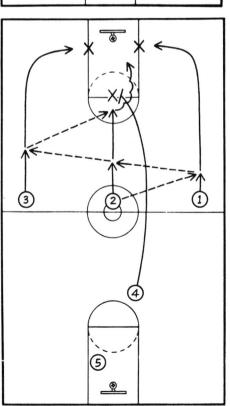

Diagram 5-13

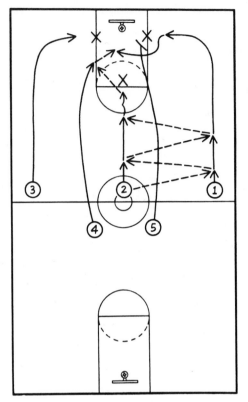

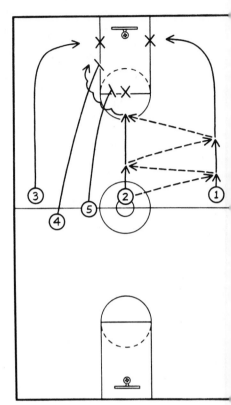

Diagram 5-14   *Diagram 5-15*

through the middle for a feed-off and score, or they may become screeners for any of the other men (Diagram 5-14). If both the screeners happen to be on the same side, they may set a double screen for 2 (Diagram 5-15).

Stopping the fast break

It is most important that the players know when to stop the fast break. The fast break should be stopped if the other players are not in favorable position to move in on the rebound, or if you do not get as good a shot attempt as you can obtain from your regular offensive patterns. This stoppage of the fast break need not be an abrupt stoppage of movement, nor a slow deliberate dribble out to the front court. It should be a continuous smooth transition into your pattern of attack. You may catch the other team in the process of getting their defense organized. This time may be a period of weakness on which you can capitalize if you are alert. The ball can always be passed to the trailers, who can decide whether to restart the pattern (Diagram 5-16). If it has gone too far, the men who were screened by the trailers can break out and start the offensive pattern (Diagram 5-17).

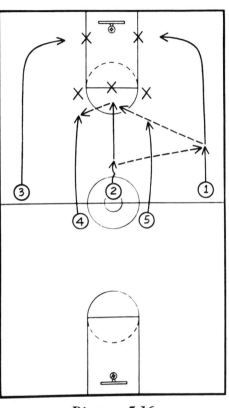

Diagram 5-16

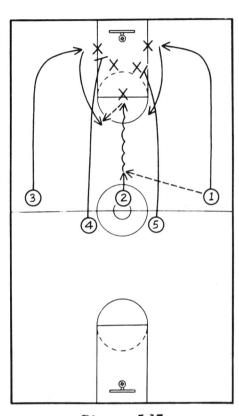

Diagram 5-17

6

Fast-Break Drills

In order to be successful with the fast-break attack, you must have players who can handle the ball well and who will work together as a team. These two qualities are just as important as speed in perfecting this style of play. The development of the fast break takes much individual and team drilling. Constant repetition of fast-break patterns and drills is a must. These basic moves must become a habit as natural as running.

Drills are hard work. Try to make them as interesting and as much fun as you can. Keep changing the drills and varying them to challenge each player. Make sure that the players do not get tired or careless in the performance of the drills. If you keep practicing fundamentals incorrectly, there will be no improvement. In fact, the bad habit will become more fixed and even more difficult to correct.

Following are a few drills which may be employed to teach and to sharpen up the fast break patterns. Many other ball-handling and fundamentals drills could be added and used.

Two-line ball-handling drill (Moving toward each other)

In the two-line ball-handling drill, split the squad into two lines in the middle of the floor. The front man in one line passes the ball to the front man in the other line and then moves on to the end of the opposite line. The ball is then passed to the next man in the opposite line and he goes to the end of that line and so on (Diagram 6-1).

The distance between the two lines can be varied and different passes may be used, such as the two-hand chest-shove pass, the bounce-pass, the one-hand handoff. This drill teaches ball-handling and movement toward the pass as you are receiving it. In order to develop the wrists and perfect ball-handling medicine balls, weighted balls, and volleyballs can be substituted for the basketball.

Two-line running drills (Moving together toward the goal)

In this drill, divide the squad into two groups under the basket at one end of the floor. The first man in each line goes toward the other goal. They pass the ball back and forth to each other, with no dribbling, while running at top speed (Diagram 6-2).

This drill teaches ball-handling at a fast pace and leading the other man with the pass as he is moving. Medicine balls, weighted balls, and volleyballs may be used to teach getting a good grip on the ball before passing it and being able to receive the ball under various circumstances.

Three-line drills (Straight down the floor)

In this drill use three lines under one basket. The first man in each line moves out. As soon as one group is halfway down the floor, the next group may start. We do not shoot on this drill. We reform the three lines at the opposite end of the court, and after everyone is at one end we start back again (Diagram 6-3).

This drill is a good combination ball-handling and conditioning drill. It teaches ball-handling at high speed and using the middle man, and helps in physical conditioning of the team (weighted balls may be used). We believe in using the ball when you run, to kill two birds with one stone. Many coaches make their players run so many laps at the end of practice. We think that drills such as this one can accomplish much more in a shorter period of time by running while passing the ball.

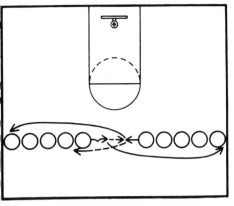

Diagram 6-1

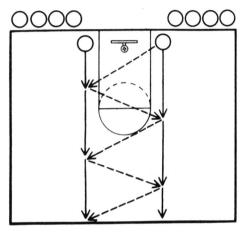

Diagram 6-2

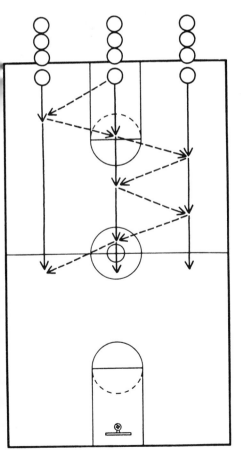

Diagram 6-3

Three-line cross drill (Cutting behind the man that you pass to)

This drill is similar to the straight-line drill, except that you change lanes, going behind the man you pass the ball to (Diagram 6-4).

This drill teaches moving toward the pass and how to change lanes if necessary, and forces the players to run at top speed in order to keep up with their teammates. It is also a good physical conditioner.

Three-lane pattern drill (No opposition)

The purpose of this drill is to learn how to go down the floor as a group and end up with the ball in position for a favorable shot from the fast break. The players do not change lanes on this drill. They go straight down the court at high speed, moving the ball back and forth with no dribbling (Diagram 6-5).

Diagram 6-4   *Diagram 6-5*

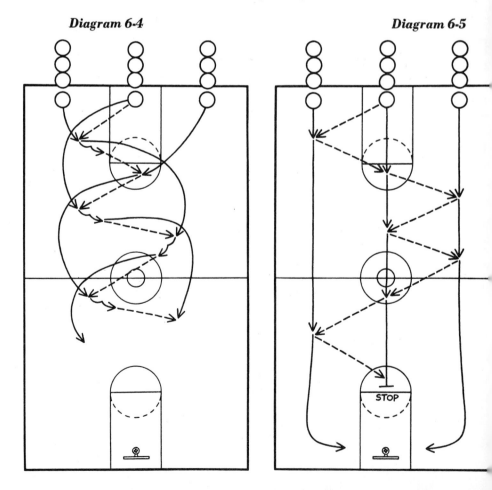

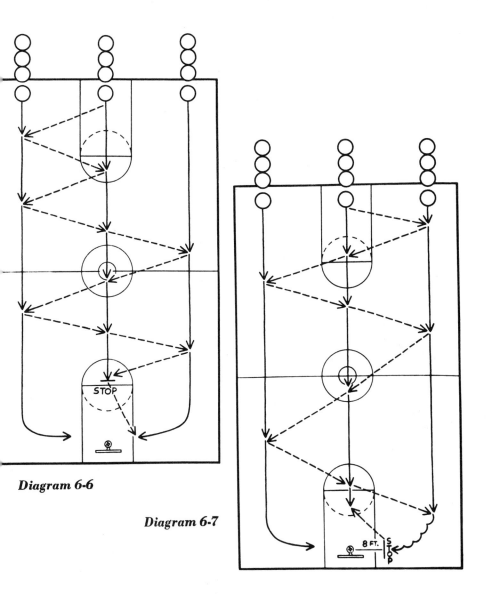

Diagram 6-6

Diagram 6-7

If the ball ends up with the middle man at or near the foul line, he *stops* and either fakes a pass and shoots a jump shot, or fakes a shot and feeds off to one of the two side men (Diagram 6-6).

If the ball ends up with one of the side men, he stops about 8 or 10 feet out along the base line. The side man can either shoot a short jumper or fake and feed off to one of the other two men who are cutting toward the goal (Diagram 6-7). After the shot, the other two men may rebound and start back down the court to the end they started from and end up with a similar situation at that end. (The man who gets the rebound will cut behind the man he passes to.) The next group can then be ready to grab the ball and go on a three-lane pattern (Diagram 6-8).

Two-on-one drills

On this drill we may use only one half of the court. One man starts out on defense and tries to cover the two men breaking for the basket. If the middle man ends up with the ball at or near the foul line he stops and either shoots a jump shot or draws out the defensive man and feeds off to the other man who is cutting for the goal (Diagram 6-9).

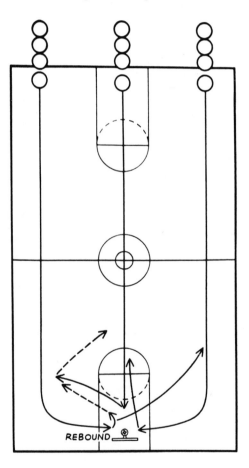

Diagram 6-8

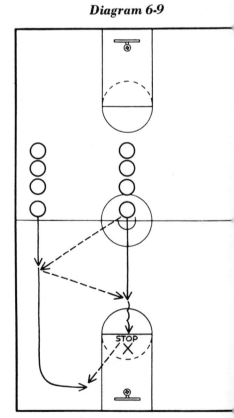

Diagram 6-9

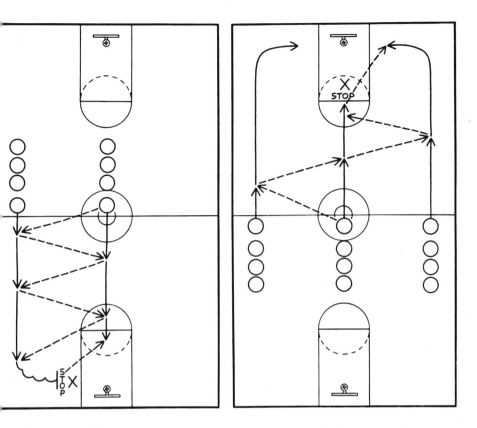

Diagram 6-10   **Diagram 6-11 Three-on-Two**

If the side man ends up with the ball, he stops eight or ten feet out and makes the defensive man commit himself to one man or the other. If the defensive man does not come out, he shoots a short jumper. If the defensive man does come out to cover him, he feeds off to the middle man (Diagram 6-10).

We run this two-lane pattern down one side or the other, and leave the outside lane open for the possible addition of the third man later. This is helpful in getting a three-on-two, if they get more help on defense.

Other half court drills (with defense)

Other half court drills may be used, applying the same principles as the two-on-one drill. Keep spread, move as a unit, make the defense commit themselves to one man, and then cash in on the advantage (Diagrams 6-11, 6-12, 6-13). (See Chapter 5 for what to do on the three-on-two, the four-on-three, and the five-on-four situations.)

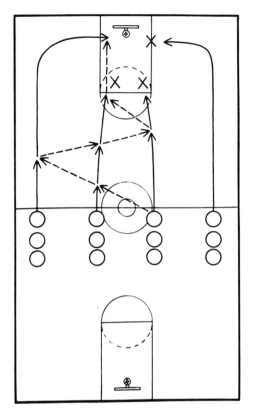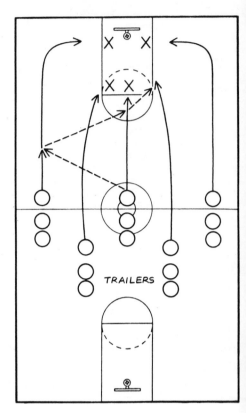

Diagram 6-12 Four-on-Three   *Diagram 6-13 Five-on-Four*

Starting the fast-break drills

One of the most important factors in the fast break is getting started quickly. If you don't get the ball and throw it out very fast to men who are forming the fast-break pattern, you can't have a fast-break attempt! These drills on starting the fast break are therefore of the utmost importance.

OFF THE DEFENSIVE REBOUND

No matter which defense we are using, we always send in three men to block out and form the rebound triangle. We also send the other two men into the circle area to play the high bounding rebounds. We practice this by having five men scatter around the floor without opposition, and the coach or manager shoots the ball against the board. As soon as the ball is in the air, the five men move into their proper rebound position (Diagram 6-14). The man who gets the ball tries to get the ball out to the side or to the middle as soon as possible (Diagram 6-15).

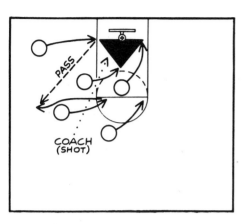

Diagram 6-14

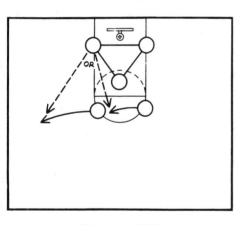

Diagram 6-15

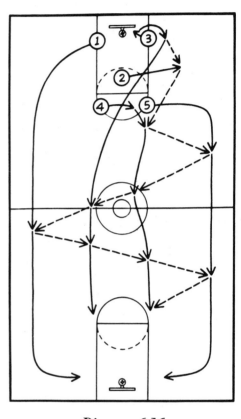

Diagram 6-16

If the rebounder can't pass to the guards, 4 and 5, on the side or middle, then he passes the ball to short pass receiver 2, and 2 will in turn try to move the ball on up the court by passing. We usually take the ball out and up the side that the rebound comes out on, unless the opposition starts to overplay our outlet passes here. The five men will go on down the floor, passing the ball back and forth as they go and end up with a three-lane fast break if the first pass went out to 4 or 5. If the first pass after the rebound went to short-pass receiver 2, they run the four-lane pattern (Diagram 6-16).

As soon as the first group of five men is across the center line, five new men are ready and move on to the floor and hit the boards on the shot by the coach or manager. When all players have gone on the fast break to one end of the court, the coach moves to the other end, and they will run the same patterns coming back up court. This practice is very good for learning to react fast to starting the fast break, and it is also a very good physical conditioner. After the patterns are learned well, opposition may be added to the drills with the addition of a two-man defense, then three-man opposition on the defensive board, then four, and finally a five-on-five situation.

OFF A FREE THROW

We practice the same drills from the free throw position. Players 1, 2, and 3 will form the rebound triangle, and 4 will block out the foul shooter from the lane and play the high bounder. Player 5 is ready to break to the side of the court that the rebound comes from or move in on a high bounding rebound. All five men are ready to play defense if they fail to get the rebound (Diagram 6-17).

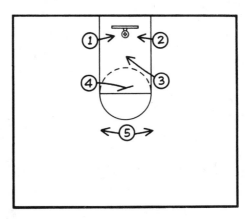

Diagram 6-17

If the rebound comes off to 1, then 5 will break to that side for a possible quick pass out, 4 will take the middle, 3 will be the short-pass receiver, and 2 will take the outside lane on the three-lane fast break (Diagram 6-18). If the pass goes to short-pass

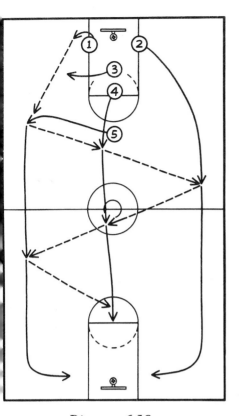 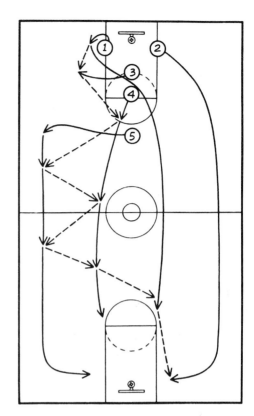

Diagram 6-18   *Diagram 6-19*

man 3, then they run the four-lane fast break (Diagram 6-19).

The same general patterns are followed on a scored free throw. One of the rebound triangle men grabs the ball out of the nets, steps out of bounds, and fires the ball to the short-pass receiver, the side man 5, or the middle man 4 (Diagram 6-20).

OFF A CONTROLLED TIP

In the defensive court, line up with three men in back of the foul circle (1, 2, and 3) and one man (5) in front. Do not start the fast-break attempt until one of your players has control of the ball. The coach may throw the ball up to 4 jumping at the foul line with no opposition (Diagram 6-21). The other players may not know who he is going to tip the ball to. If he tips the ball to 3, then 5 will break to that side for the first pass, and 2 will go up the middle. Player 1 (after he sees that we have the ball) may fill the third lane, and 4 and 3 will come in as trailers (Diagram 6-22).

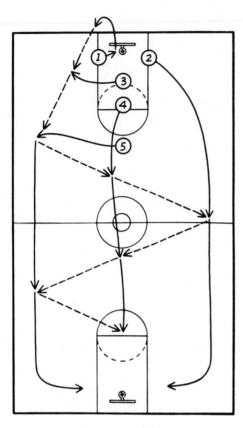

Diagram 6-20

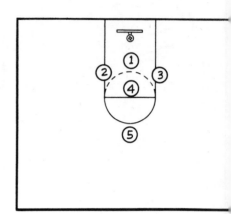

Diagram 6-21

Diagram 6-22

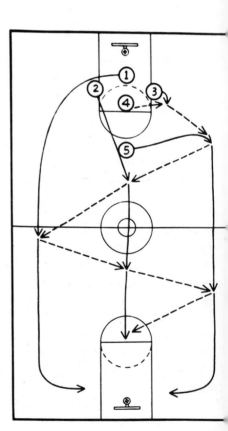

If the ball goes to 2, then 5 breaks to that side of the floor, and 3 will take the middle lane. Player 1 will fill the outside lane, and 2 and 4 will come in as trailers (Diagram 6-23).

If the ball is tipped to 5, then 2 and 3 fill the side lines and go on the three-lane fast break. Players 1 and 4 will come in as trailers (Diagram 6-24).

On this drill, as soon as one group has gone on the fast-break attempt five new men can move into defensive tipping position. The coach throws up the ball, the tipper may tip to any man, and a new group forms. After all men have gone the coach may move to the other end of the floor and the groups may run the drill back up court.

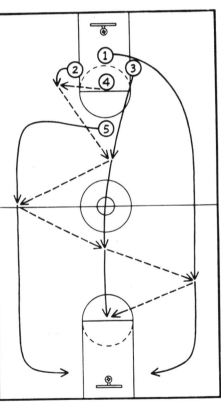

Diagram 6-24

Diagram 6-23

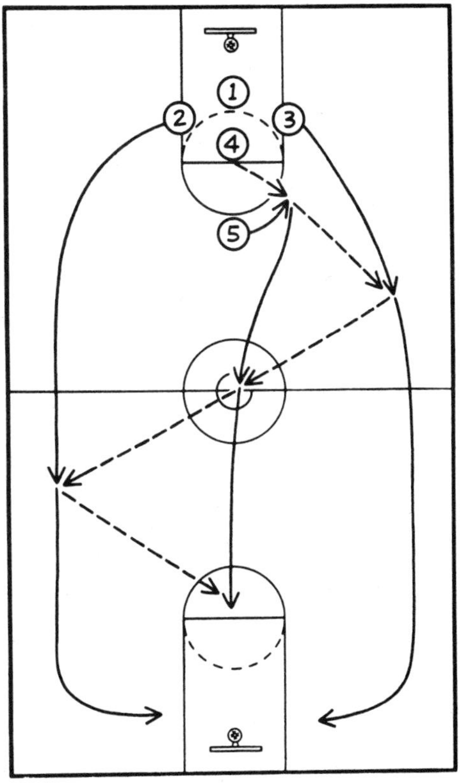

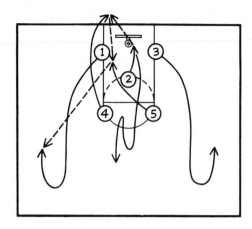

Diagram 6-25

AGAINST A FULL-COURT PRESS

The coach may have five men ready to run the "fast-break-off-a-rebound drill" and instead lay the ball in the basket and call "press." Against a full-court press, we try to get the ball to mid-court fast and outnumber the back court men, before the down-court pressers can get back on defense. Players 1, 2, and 3 break up toward the center line and then reverse if necessary. Player 4 takes the ball players 1, 2, or 3 gets the ball out of the net and quickly throws it out to 4, who looks to pass in to 5 or else back to 1, 2, or 3 (Diagram 6-25). (See Chapter 4 for full details.)

ON A SCORED GOAL

On a scored field goal or free throw an inside man may take the ball out of the net, step back, and fire the ball up court to start a fast-break attempt. If 2 gets the ball, he steps out and 1 will be the short-pass receiver while 4 and 5 will break into the side and middle spots. Player 3 will take the outside lane (see Chapter 4). The coach may work this drill in with the "fast-break-off-a-free-throw drill" or "fast-break-off-a-rebound drill" (Diagram 6-26).

FILLING-THE-LANES DRILL

The aim of this drill is to learn to move into the fast-break position and to fill the three lanes as soon as possible, no matter where the players happen to be on the floor. Five men mill around on the floor, changing position frequently. When the coach shoots the ball, the three men nearest the goal move in to form the rebound triangle and the other two men move to the high bounding rebound position. For the sake of this drill, we assume that one man did not get into his lane. The middle man

70

must assume this position, and nearest man must fill the middle lane, next nearest man must assume the outside lane (Diagram 6-27). The man closest to the rebounder will be the short-pass receiver.

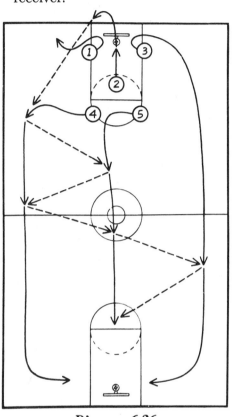

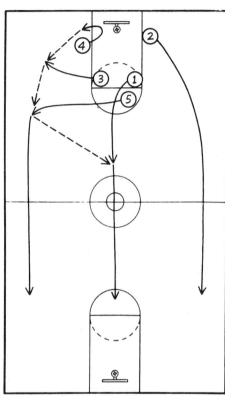

Diagram 6-26   *Diagram 6-27*

CAN'T-PASS DRILL

On the fast break we always try to pass the ball up court if possible. If we can't pass the ball we dribble. Any time that an outside man can't pass to the middle man because he is covered he will drive to the middle lane, the middle man will cross over into his outside lane (Diagram 6-28).

If the middle man can't pass to either side, then he may dribble to one of the outside lanes, and the outside man will then assume the middle lane (Diagram 6-29). On this drill, we may let two defensive men over-play two of the offensive men in the three lanes, thus forcing the dribble and cross of the lanes.

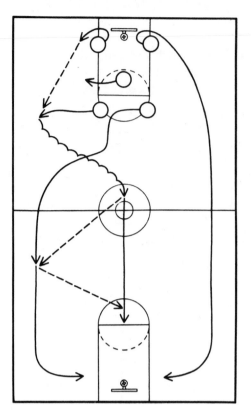

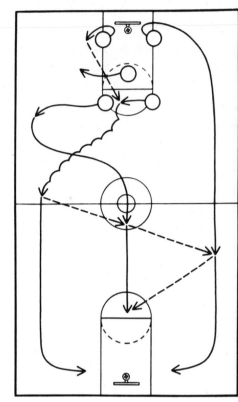

Diagram 6-28   **Diagram 6-29**

Competitive Team Drills

After we have learned the fast-break positions and what to do on the fast break in the various situations, we may run a five-on-five drill. The offensive team is given the ball at one end of the court and may run our regular offensive patterns. If the offensive team scores, they get two points and *also get to keep the ball* and set up another play. The only way that the defensive team can get the ball back is to get a rebound, or steal the ball, and make a good fast-break attempt. If they are successful in doing this, they become the offensive team. The team which allowed the fast break must then stay on defense until they can get the ball and start a successful fast-break attempt. If they get a rebound and fail to get a fast break started, then they must give up the ball. The score is kept on the scoreboard, and the team with the most points at the end of ten minutes is the winner. Quite often this drill may replace our regular scrimmage.

7

Getting the Ball to Start
the Fast Break

In order to make rabbit stew,
you must first catch a rabbit. In order to have a fast break, you
must first get the ball. As soon as the Triple-Threat team loses
the ball they should plot to get the ball back again and prevent
the other team from scoring.

There are several ways to regain possession of the ball. (1)
Force the other team to take a bad or off-balance shot and then
gain the rebound. (2) Get a double-teaming situation and force a
tie-up or a steal. (3) Play your defense so that you can play the
passing lanes and possibly deflect or steal a pass. (4) Be so
aggressive with a press defense that you shock or excite the other
team into making offensive errors. (5) Play so tight a zone
defense that the other team cannot penetrate the middle and is
forced to take long or hurried shots, on which you can control the
boards.

The worst things you can do in trying to regain possession of
the ball are to commit careless or foolish fouls and to give the

other team good shots at the basket. The Triple-Threat team must learn the secret of balancing the drive to get the ball back with a good, sound defense. This lesson is one of the keys to the success or failure of your defensive attack.

The importance of rebounding

One of the best times to start a fast-break attempt is after a defensive rebound. If you do not have aggressive rebounders who take personal pride in this phase of the game it is very difficult to use the fast break as one of your offensive weapons.

The coach should be happy when he hears his players discussing the game in the dressing room and they are asking questions such as: "How many rebounds did I get?" "How many points did I hold my man to?" "How many rebounds did my man get?" Desire and attitude are important factors in rebounding. Good rebounders do not always get their names in the paper, but winning teams always seem to have several of them around.

Rebounding form

Rebounding can be learned! It is not an inherited trait but is acquired by hard work, desire, and personal pride. Size and jumping ability are assets in rebounding but they do not assure possession of the rebound. The inside men must learn to think rebound and to move in on the board as if they owned it.

On the defensive board the player must learn to spread out his arms and legs after a rebound, and keep his opponent off the board; then he must give himself plenty of room to move in on the ball wherever it comes off the rim or board. On the offensive board, the rebounder must learn to get around the man who is trying to block him out, or to lead his man deep under the goal and then play the rebound over his head.

Rebound form should start with the release of the ball by the other team. The men who are guarding men who did not shoot the ball should start to spread-eagle and keep an eye on their man and the ball at the same time. They should then move in their proper rebound positions.

The man guarding the shooter should watch both his man and the ball, anticipate where the shooter is going, and then beat him there. He should then block him out and be ready tó move in on the ball. The rebounder should let the man that he is trying to block out make the first contact, not back up into his man. If he watches the shooter he will often get a tip as to where the rebound is going.

The rebounder should move to meet the rebound and should jump at the proper time to meet the ball as high as possible in the air. He must be sure that the ball is on its downward flight and is not still going up, but if he waits for the ball to come down into his arms, it may never get there.

The rebounder should learn to grab the ball with both hands and pull it down with force. He should learn to jack-knife and come down with a good spread, with the knees bent and the elbows out to protect the ball. As soon as he gets the ball, he should be looking for someone to get the first pass out to, in order to keep from being tied up and to get an advantage on the fast break.

Importance of positioning and timing

The secrets of rebounding are proper positioning and timing. Good rebounders seem to have the knack of being at the right place at the right time. This knack comes from learning to get good position and proper timing on the jump. A smaller player with good jumping ability plus good positioning and timing can become a very good rebounder. He can often be several inches taller on the basketball court than he appears in his street shoes. A big man who has these qualities can "own the board."

In positioning, the defensive rebounder must turn part way in order to see both his man and the ball at the same time. He must keep his man as far away from the rebound area as possible. It is a cardinal sin to be caught too far under the goal to get the rebound, and to have it bound over your head to the opponent. On the offensive board the rebounder must learn to fight around his man or fake a move into one rebound position and then reverse into another position. Try to take your defensive man in under the goal and then block him out from the high bounder.

Proper timing must be learned in order to get the ball at its peak. If you jump too soon you will be going up with the ball on the rebound and therefore will be coming down as the ball is coming down. You will be standing on the floor when the ball is in your reach. If you jump too late, someone else will have already picked the ball out of mid-air. Time the jump to meet the ball just as it has started on its downward arch. Being able to jump well is of little value unless you have the skill of proper timing. Proper timing takes practice.

Blocking out on the rebound

There are two methods used to block out on the defensive rebound. One is the man-to-man block-out and the other is a zone block-out. Most teams use the man-to-man check-out with a man-to-man defense and the zone method with their zone defense.

With the man-to-man method each player is responsible for the man that he is guarding and must make a legal block-out on each rebound. The theory is that if each player takes care of his man on the rebound, the opposing team cannot possibly get the ball. If one man fails to block out his man, then he greatly lessens his own team's chances of getting the rebound.

With the zone block-out method, each player is responsible for a definite area on the floor. The three inside men form a rebound triangle, and the two guards play the high bounding rebounds (see Chapter 4). Each player must be responsible for his area and he must not allow an offensive rebounder to penetrate his zone.

Rules for getting the rebound

Any size basketball team can learn to get their share of rebounds. Much individual and team practice time must be spent in making rebounding knowledge into rebounding habit. Following are a few important points which must be remembered:

1. Step away from your offensive man with the shot to look the situation over.
2. Try to watch your man and the ball at the same time. (See if he tips you off as to where the ball is going to go.)
3. Look to see which way your man wants to go and then get in front of him.
4. Do not back into your man. Make the offensive man make the contact.
5. Spread-eagle, get your arms up, and take up as much room on the floor as possible.
6. Know where the ball is and then move in to claim it.

7. Jump when you can get the ball at the peak of your jump—get as high in the air as you possibly can.
8. Grab the ball with two hands and pull it down with force.
9. Spread your legs as you grab the ball in order to give yourself room to come down on the floor. (This will prevent many sprained ankles, because you will have a solid base to land on.)
10. Protect the ball after you come down by bending at the waist and getting your elbows out.
11. Do not stand and admire your good fortune in gaining possession of the ball. Look down the floor and get the first pass out as soon as possible.
12. Make sure that you have done your part in your over-all plan to regain possession of the ball. If each man does his job well your team will get a good share of the rebounds. Rebounding should be a team effort.

Individual timing and jumping drills

Many drills can be devised to help the individual player improve his timing and jumping ability. One of the best for timing is simply to work several minutes before and after formal practice in tipping the ball against the board eight or ten times and then tipping it in the basket. Make sure that the player is getting high in the air and is meeting the ball at the peak of his jump. He should not go up and down with the ball, but he must keep the ball up as high as possible. He should work with each hand separately and with both hands.

The jump-rope is a very valuable tool in improving timing and foot work. Each player should use the jump-rope for a few minutes each day. This is also a good conditioner and can help improve muscular co-ordination.

Another individual drill can be jumping at the rim. The player moves in from one side and tries to see how much of his hand or arm that he can get over the rim of the basket. He should come in from all angles and make sure that he "high-jumps" and not "broad-jumps" at the goal. Make sure that the players do not grab hold of the rim. If a player is too short to touch the goal, he can jump at the net or at the backboard.

Jump-reach test

One of the first tests that we give our players is the jump-reach test. This is a simple test but it is a good indicator of jumping ability. The player is given a small piece of chalk and told to make a mark on the wall as high as he can reach without getting his feet off of the floor. He then squats and leaps as high into the air as he can reach and makes a mark on the wall as high as possible. The distance between the two marks is measured and recorded (anything over 30 inches is excellent).

This test can become competitive and players can work to improve their performance during the year. Tests should be recorded several times during the year and any improvement noted.

Circle-tip drill

The purpose of this drill is to teach timing, jumping ability, fingertip control, and proper wrist action in tipping the ball.

Five players line up around the circle with one man at the foul line and the other four around the circle. The center man throws up the ball and tips it to any of the other four players. They in turn tip it back to any other man (Diagram 7-1). The center position is alternated every few minutes. Later two basketballs can be used in this drill to speed up the action.

Three-man tipping drill

This drill is to develop timing, jumping ability, and fingertip control of the ball. Three men form a triangle around the basket. One of them throws the ball against the board for one of the other

Diagram 7-1   *Diagram 7-2*

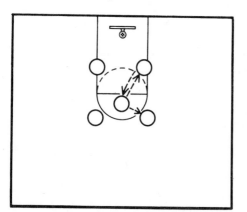
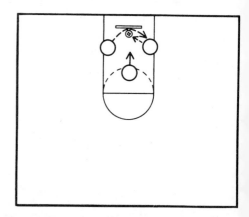

men to tip into the basket. Stress meeting the ball as high in the air as possible and do not allow slapping of the ball (Diagram 7-2). The positions should be alternated, and the players should learn to use both left and right hands.

One-on-one rebound drill

The purpose of this drill is to teach blocking-out on defense. It also teaches the offensive rebounder to fake and try to get position on the defensive man. Stress that the defensive man should own the rebound. If he fails to get it, he may be penalized by running a lap around the gym floor. This can become a very competitive drill.

The squad is divided into two lines. One line is under the goal and the other at the back of the circle. The ball is given to the first man in line at the circle, who drives into the foul circle and shoots a jump shot. The first man in the line under the goal rushes out to stop the shooter and then must turn and block him out from the rebound. Stress keeping the offensive man out as far as possible until he moves in to claim the rebound (Diagram 7-3). You can also let the players challenge each other to see who can get the most defensive and the most offensive rebounds.

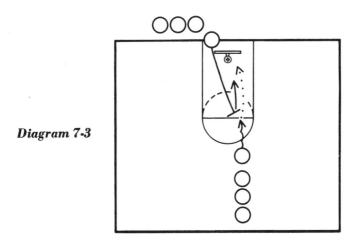

Diagram 7-3

Three-on-three rebounding drill

On this drill the squad is divided into three-man teams. Both ends of the basketball court may be used. One group of three is designated as the defensive team and another group of three as

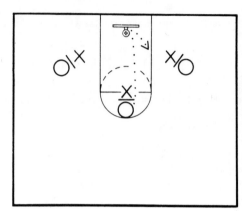

Diagram 7-4　　　　　　　　　　　　　**Diagram 7-5**

offensive. The offensive team tries to score on short jump shots. The defensive team plays them man-to-man and must block out after the shot for the rebound (Diagram 7-4).

We stress good defense and blocking out for the rebound. Each player must do his job on defense and in rebounding. In order to illustrate that the failure of one man to do his job can affect the entire team, the defensive squad, if they are scored upon or if they fail to get the rebound, must all run a lap around the gym floor.

To stress blocking out, we sometimes do not rebound on this drill. We just block the offensive men out so far that the ball is allowed to hit the floor from the rebound (Diagram 7-5).

Five-man-team rebound drill

In this five-on-five drill, we try to make the rebound situation game-like and very competitive. Five men are designated as offense and take the outside positions. Five men are designated as defense and take the inside positions. The coach or manager dribbles the ball out court and then shoots the ball from any angle. The defensive men must block out their opponents and

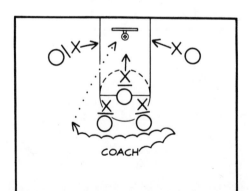

Diagram 7-6

control the rebound (Diagram 7-6). The team that controls the rebound is given one point. Ten shots are taken, and then the offensive and defensive teams exchange positions. Ten more shots are taken, and the team which has the most points is challenged by a new group. The losing squad must go to the other end of the court and run rebound drills for five minutes.

Both zone and man-to-man rebounding positioning may be used with this drill. Also, you can practice starting the fast break off the defensive rebound with this drill. You can make a rule that in order for the defensive rebounder to get his team a point, he must get the first pass out to one of his men breaking into the rebounding position very quickly. If he does not make a pass out in less than two seconds, he may lose his point for rebounding. If the rebounder is tied up after he brings the ball down, he may lose his point. The team which prevents the quick pass out or makes the tie-up is then awarded the point.

Use of rebounding devices

There are many commercial rebounding devices on the market which are excellent teaching aids for rebounding. Some are wall mounted, and some are on rollers and are portable. Most of them have a ball, the altitude of which can be varied, and which must be pulled down with force. They are very helpful in increasing jumping ability and learning to get a good hold on the ball.

Many home made devices can be created by the coach to act as teaching aids. Rings may be placed in the goal to make the opening smaller. Canvas or rubber sheeting can be stretched over the goal for use in rebounding and tipping practice.

A basketball can be suspended from a long rope and hung over the backboard, over a metal rod or support, or across a steel girder. One player or manager can keep a hold on the rope and control the force with which the rebounder must pull the ball down.

Competitive drills can be created with the aid of these devices, and a player can take personal pride in being able to show improvement in his jumping ability throughout the season.

Cross-block drill

On the offensive board players are often blocked out from the rebound. In order to counteract this, we often use a cross-block on the offensive rebound.

If the shot is taken by a guard the three inside men rotate their positions clock-wise, with each man getting the inside position on the other player's defensive man (Diagram 7-7).

If the shot is taken by a forward on the side, then the other two inside men change positions and get the inside rebounding position. The guards play the high bounding rebound and are ready to fall back on defense (Diagram 7-8).

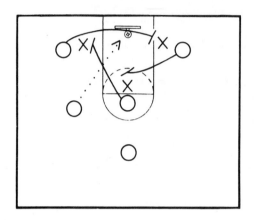

Diagram 7-7

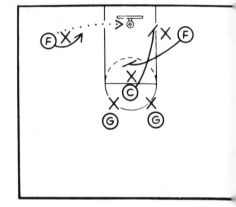

Diagram 7-8

Deflecting the pass drill

With the aggressive man-to-man defense and the press defense we try to play both the man and the passing lanes. In this drill we practice timing and quickness in deflecting passes.

We set up a three-on-three situation out court, with three offensive men and three defensive men. The point man is given the ball and is covered by one defensive man. The other two defensive men not only try to guard their men, but also try to keep their men from even receiving a pass. They try to play both the man and the passing lane at the same time (Diagram 7-9).

The back two guards must be very alert and not let their men make a quick cut for the basket. When the ball is passed they are alert for an opportunity to deflect the pass. They attempt to keep their men from receiving a pass. If the pass does go to the side man, then the point defensive man must play both the man and

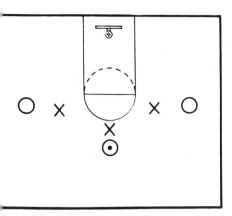
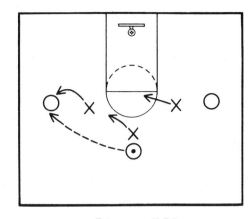

| Diagram 7-9 | Diagram 7-10 |

the passing lanes. The side man will then play his man tight man-to-man as the other men sag. Defensive men must be alert for screens and picks, as well as quick cuts for the goal (Diagram 7-10).

Learning to deflect the pass to where a teammate can pick it up is not an easy task. It takes quickness and constant alertness, and a lot of hard work to perfect it. If your players do not have these skills do not attempt to use these defensive maneuvers.

8

Developing the Perpetual-
Pattern Offense

Offense is only one phase of the
game of basketball. Some coaches have the philosophy that if
you have a good offense the defense will take care of itself.
Others are of the opposite opinion. We have found that no phase
of the game of basketball will take care of itself. All phases of the
game must be well-planned and practiced, if they are to be used
successfully.

The most important factors in team offense are organization
and individual fundamentals. A team with a well-organized
attack and good individual offensive fundamentals will be successful with any offensive plan. Offense is where many coaches
over-coach their players. If he is not winning, he is ready to
change their plays or adopt some other team's offensive style of
play. Some teams have so many set plays that they never really
use any of them effectively. The players become so confused on
offense that they stand and watch the game. They wait for something to happen—and of course it never does.

Any plan of attack must move in order to be successful. It must involve more than one or two players. Players without the ball must learn to move and work hard to get open. A slow-motion offense can never be successful. The more moves which an offensive pattern makes, the more chances there are for the defense to commit an error. It is these defensive errors that the offense is working and waiting to take advantage of and is ready to turn into points on the scoreboard.

The importance of individual offensive fundamentals

An offensive plan can only be as good as the individuals who are working it. If you do not have sound individual offensive fundamentals you can not possibly have a good team offensive attack. Boys with sound fundamentals can make any offense look great. Weak fundamentals can make the best offensive plans look poor. All players must know how to pivot, cut, screen, roll, dribble, pass, fake, drive, and shoot. They must not only know how to do these things but also when to do them.

Many players will work for hours in shooting practice and neglect working on how to get their shots. If they are unable to maneuver to obtain their shots, this fine shooting ability is of little value to the team. If a player's shooting is off, it is not always because of his shooting ability. It may be in how he is taking his shot or when he is shooting the ball. A player must be able to hit when he gets his shot on the offense, but there is much more to playing offense than just being able to shoot.

The idea of the perpetual-pattern offense

The perpetual-pattern offense is never really stopped, it is only slowed down. In the perpetual pattern there is always an alternative if one play does not work out. If the first play attempt is successful and you get a good shot (where the shooter has a 50-50 or better chance of scoring) you may shoot in just a few seconds. If the play does not work you move right on to a second. If you don't get the good shot you move on to the third, and so on.

At times you may shoot in 15-25 seconds. At other times you may have to work for one or two or more minutes. The important thing is to shoot any time you get the percentage shot, and not to shoot the low percentage shot at any time. With the perpetual pattern there is a certain amount of freedom to take advantage of the defense at any time. The perpetual-pattern team must be patient and diligent in their play, but they must avoid stagnation.

They must keep their offense in constant motion. Many teams move very well when they first get the ball on offense, but slow down or stop altogether if the first play or pattern is not successful. The success of a play or pattern depends not only on the soundness of the play itself, but also on how the play or pattern is executed.

The step-by-step development of the offense

The offense should be developed slowly. Each phase should become habit before moving on to new dimensions. Start with simple individual moves and two- and three-man plays. Then move on to the more involved team play.

With afternoon and evening classes we sometimes have a difficult time getting all of the team members at practice at the same time. In any school academic work must come first. We build and schedule our practice sessions around classwork.

This means that we must have many individual exercises and drills which can be used by the individual or by small groups of players. You might say that we have prefabricated plays which can be put together in a hurry whenever we do get all the players together at one time.

With the perpetual pattern the players must learn to execute the proper moves and plays at the proper time. They must learn to take advantage of all individual or team weaknesses which are observed. It is foolish to run a play just for the sake of the play. The players must learn to take advantage of all weaknesses no matter when they occur.

Many teams feel that they must run a play to perfection to score the two points. This is a fine ideal, but if the other team over-plays your pattern you must learn to use the back door and take the advantage. You should be able to adapt your plays or patterns to the other team, and still be able to take advantage of their over-play and score on their defensive weakness. This is one of the great advantages of having a well-organized attack. As the opposition is concentrating on stopping your organized team attack you concentrate on looking for individual defensive errors.

One-on-one moves

Every man on the team must be a threat to score with a one-on-one situation. If one player has a definite edge on the man who is guarding him, we may try to get the ball to him and then clear out to give him room to move on the one-on-one. There are many ways for a man to get a good scoring opportunity with a clear-cut one-on-one situation.

1. Fake a shot and draw your man close enough to drive, either left or right, for a jump shot or a lay-up. Use your eyes to fake with and watch the defensive man at all times with peripheral vision. Make the defensive man commit himself and then take the advantage.
2. Fake a pass to pull the defense to one side or the other and then drive on the weak side. Fake with your head and shoulders and not with the ball.
3. Use the rocker step—fake the start of a drive by thrusting one foot forward and then rocking back on your pivot foot. If the defensive man backs up, you have room to shoot a good jump or set shot. If the defense recovers and moves toward you, you can fake the shot and drive in either direction.
4. Use the rocker step and draw the defense close to you. Then turn the back to the defense and use a fake reverse and drive on the opposite side.
5. Start your dribble and take the defensive man as deep toward the goal or base line as you can. If you can get him moving backward, you can stop and shoot the jumper.
6. Start the dribble, stop quickly, and execute a reverse pivot for a close-in jump shot or a possible feed-off to a man cutting into your original position. When you stop, protect the ball well and do not hold it out in front of the defense.
7. Use the change-of-pace dribble. Start fast, slow down, mark time and then go again, faking and feinting with eyes, head, and shoulders as you go.
8. Use the change of direction. You can start the dribble fast, then stop and reverse. Change dribbling hands with your back to the defensive player. Fake and reverse, or else double fake and go.
9. Use any combination of the above individual maneuvers. If you are stopped on the dribble, do not keep the ball, but get it to one of your teammates as soon as possible.

Two-man plays

Basic parts of the perpetual-pattern offense may be worked on and developed with small groups of individuals. Two-man plays can be run with any two or four individuals present. You can run guard-guard plays, guard-forward plays, or guard-pivot plays according to which men are available at a given time. Against these plays you can use man-to-man defense and work on offensive and defensive fundamentals at the same time.

Guard-Forward Plays

To start the guard-forward plays, the forward is deep on one side, about six or seven feet from the base line and about the same distance from the side line. He may rove about to the base line and back up. The guard is to the side and at the top of the key (Diagram 8-1). The basic options do not go by numbers. The players learn to execute them by habit according to the way that the defense covers them

Option 1 (Diagram 8-2): The forward fakes and breaks toward the mid line of the court on the side. The guard passes to the forward meeting the ball and can cut to the outside for a possible return pass.

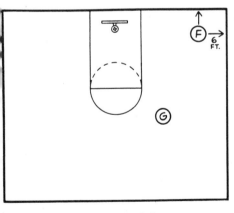

Diagram 8-1

Diagram 8-2

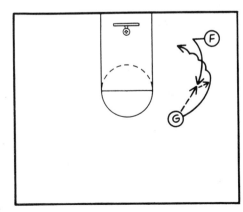

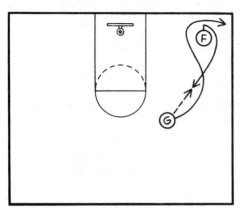

Diagram 8-4

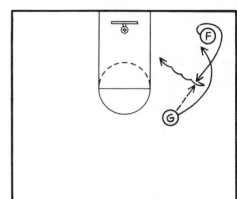

Diagram 8-3

Option 2 (Diagram 8-3): If the guard does not get the return pass he can button-hook back to the corner for a pass and a possible shot, or drive from the corner. (The forward could also go to the corner, to screen for the guard in the corner.)

Option 3 (Diagram 8-4): The forward can fake a hand-off to the guard and pivot to the inside for a drive or a possible jump shot.

Option 4 (Diagram 8-5): The forward can fake the pass-off, dribble to the inside, and hit the guard cutting for the basket.

Option 5 (Diagram 8-6): The forward can hand off to the guard and then roll for the basket for a return pass.

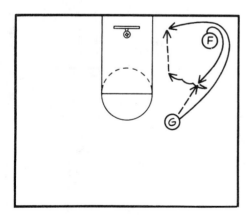

Diagram 8-6

Diagram 8-5

Option 6 (Diagram 8-7): The guard can cut to the inside instead of the outside for a hand-off. (We may have a signal for this.)

Option 7 (Diagram 8-8): The forward may turn and roll after the hand-off for a possible return pass.

Option 8 (Diagram 8-9): The guard can cut to the inside and screen for a drive or jump shot by the forward.

Option 9 (Diagram 8-10): The forward can fake the use of the screen and go to the outside instead.

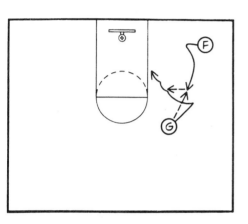

Diagram 8-7

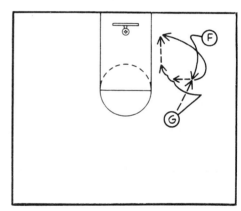

Diagram 8-8

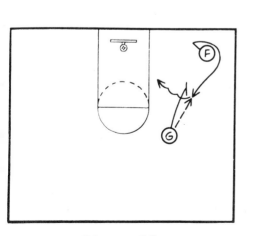

Diagram 8-9

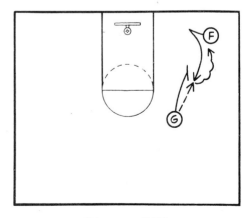

Diagram 8-10

Option 10 (Diagram 8-11): After the inside screen the guard can roll toward the goal for a possible return pass.

Option 11 (Diagram 8-12): Instead of cutting to the outside or the inside, the guard can elect not to cut. If the guard does not cut, the forward fires the ball back to him and screens his man.

Option 12 (Diagram 8-13): After the screen, the forward can roll toward the goal for a possible return pass.

Option 13 (Diagram 8-14): If the forward is covered when he gets to the mid-line then he may screen for the guard. (The forward can also roll after the screen.)

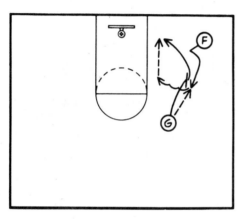

Diagram 8-11

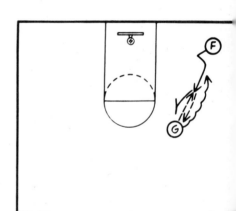

Diagram 8-12

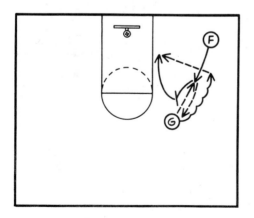

Diagram 8-13

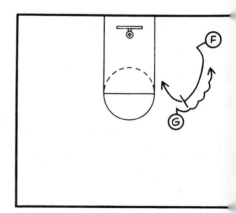

Diagram 8-14

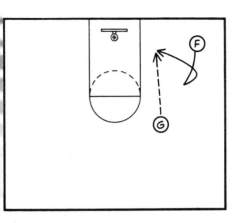

Diagram 8-15

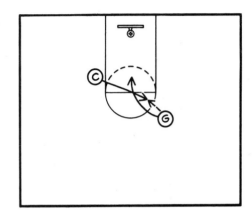

Diagram 8-16

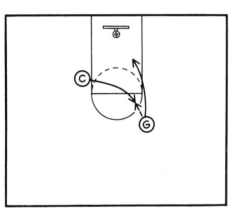

Diagram 8-17

Option 14 (Diagram 8-15): If the forward's defensive man starts to cover his break for the mid-line he can fake a break and then reverse and cut for the goal for an easy lay-up shot.

GUARD-PIVOT PLAYS

When the guard passes in to the pivot there are several options which he may choose. First of all, he can screen for the other guard or for the forward on his side of the floor. On the two-man plays, he can pass and cut on either side of the pivot man. (*Options 1 and 2*, Diagrams 8-16, 8-17).

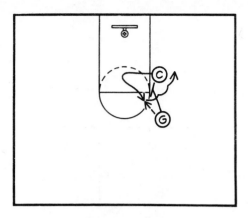

Diagram 8-18

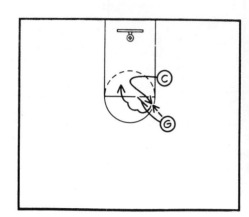

Diagram 8-19

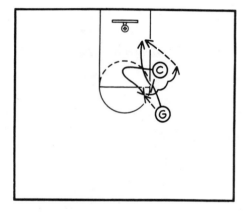

Diagram 8-20

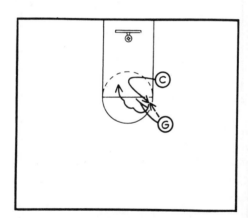

Diagram 8-21

Options 3 and 4 (Diagram 8-18, 8-19): If the pivot man receives the ball on the side of the key, the guard can screen for him on either side. The pivot man can come around the screen for a jump shot or drive for the goal.

Option 5 and 6 (Diagram 8-20, 8-21): After the screen the guard can roll toward the basket for a possible return pass.

94

Options 7 and 8 (Diagrams 8-22, 8-23): The guard can also cut hard, then reverse, and cut around the pivot on either side.

Option 9 (Diagram 8-24): The guard can pass into the pivot and take his man into the key, as if he were going to cut through. The guard stops and the pivot man feeds the ball back to the guard. He then sets a screen on the guard's defensive man. This sets up the mismatch in the key area, as the guard uses the screen. The defensive pivot man must pick up the guard. The guard can feed the ball back to the pivot man cutting down the lane.

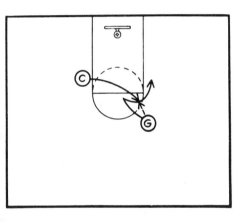

Diagram 8-22

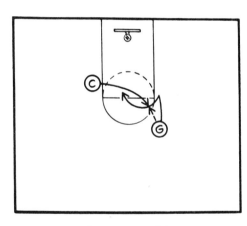

Diagram 8-23

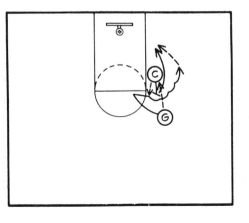

Diagram 8-24

GUARD-GUARD PLAYS

Before starting some plays, the guards may have to wait for the inside men to break into the proper position to receive the pass-in from the outer key area. They can cross or start the guard-guard options.

Option 1 (Diagram 8-25): The guard with the ball can fake a pass inside and fire the ball to the other guard; then he can break down the center for a return pass.

Option 2 (Diagram 8-26): The guard can pass and then screen for the other guard.

Option 3 (Diagram 8-27): After the screen, the guard can roll for the basket.

Option 4 (Diagram 8-28): The guard can pass to the other guard and then cut on the back side.

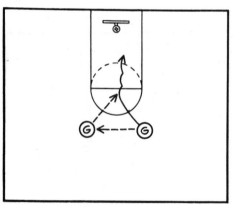

Diagram 8-25   Diagram 8-26

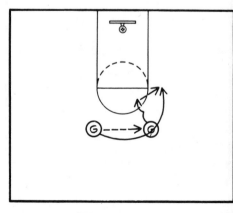

Diagram 8-27   **Diagram 8-28**

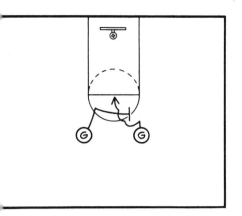 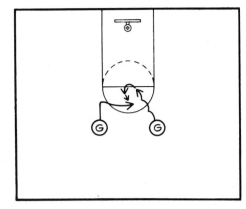

| Diagram 8-29 | Diagram 8-30 |

Option 5 (Diagram 8-29): The guard without the ball can fake a cut and then come to screen for the man with the ball. (He can roll after the pick.)

Option 6 (Diagram 8-30): The guard with the ball can start the dribble and pull the defense in. He can then stop and make a reverse pivot and the other guard can cut around him for a hand-off pass or jump shot.

Three-man plays

After all of the two-man plays have been learned and developed so that they are habit and can be used effectively, then we may add a third man to the pattern. You may run three-man plays with two guards and a forward; one guard, one forward, and a pivot man; or two guards and a pivot man.

GUARD-GUARD-FORWARD PLAYS

The plays with two guards and a forward are the same as the two man guard-guard plays and the guard-forward plays. The guards may start a guard-guard play and not get the opening. They then throw the ball back out to the forward to continue play. One guard can pass to the forward and then screen for the other guard. One guard can pass to the other guard and then screen for the forward.

GUARD-GUARD-PIVOT PLAYS

With the addition of the pivot man, you may start a guard-guard two man play and then involve the pivot man with a guard-pivot play. If the guard-pivot play does not work out, then the ball can be passed back out to the other guard to continue play. You may run as many options as you like before taking the shot.

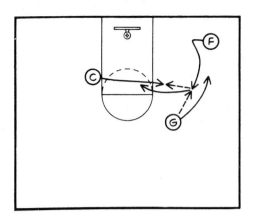

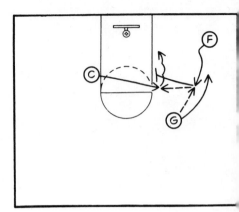

Diagram 8-31   Diagram 8-32

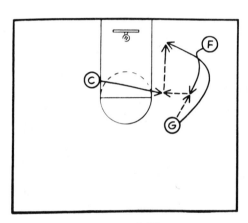

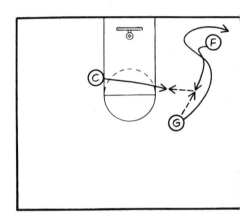

Diagram 8-33   Diagram 8-34

GUARD-FORWARD-PIVOT PLAYS

On these plays you can use the guard-pivot or guard-forward two-man plays and also involve the third man.

Option 1 (Diagram 8-31): The guard passes the ball in to the forward and breaks to his outside. The forward fakes a hand-off to the guard, who is cutting, and then feeds in to the pivot man, who has set up on the side of the key. The forward can then cut on either side of the pivot man.

Option 2 (Diagram 8-32): The same three-man play can be executed with the forward, instead of cutting, setting a screen for the pivot man to roll around.

Option 3 (Diagram 8-33): The guard can pass to the forward and cut to the outside. The forward can fake a hand-off and then pass to the pivot man coming across the lane. The pivot man can hit the guard who is breaking for the goal.

Option 4 (Diagram 8-34): If there is a delay on the pass from the pivot man in Option 3, then the guard cutting for the goal can button-hook to the corner.

Option 5 (Diagram 8-35): The guard can pass in to the pivot man and then split the post with the forward cutting from the side.

Option 6 (Diagram 8-36): The guard can pass to the pivot and then screen for the forward to roll around. (After the screen the guard can roll for the basket also.)

Option 7 (Diagram 8-37): The guard can pass in to the forward and then set a screen for the pivot man.

Option 8 (Diagram 8-38): The pivot man can set a screen for the forward. The guard can pass to the forward, cutting around the screen.

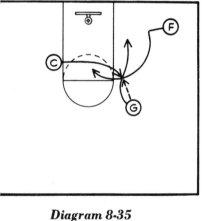

Diagram 8-35

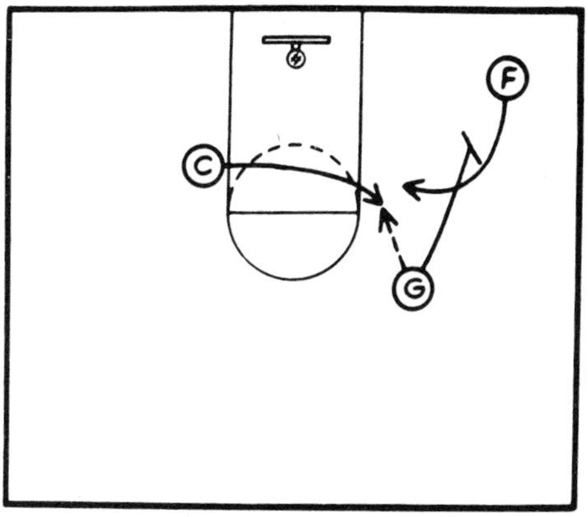

Diagram 8-36

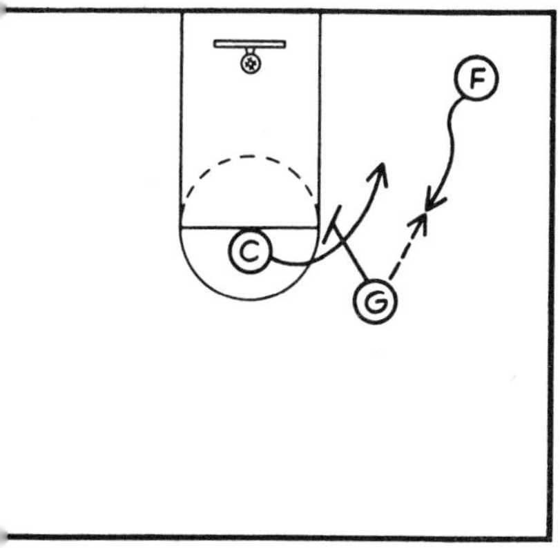

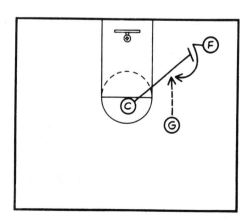

Diagram 8-37

Diagram 8-38

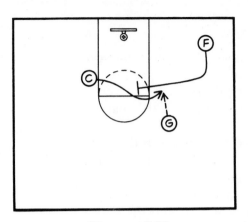

Diagram 8-39

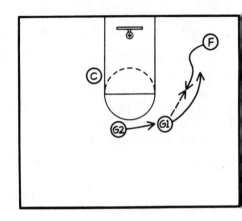

Diagram 8-40

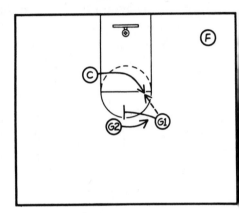

Diagram 8-41

Diagram 8-42

Option 9 (Diagram 8-39): The forward can cut and then screen for the pivot man. The guard then passes in to the pivot man. (The guard can also cut or screen after his pass.)

Four-man plays

After you have fully developed the two-and three-man plays, you can move on to plays which involve a fourth player. The same principles apply as with the two- and three-man plays. You can run the plays with any four players, omitting a guard, a forward, or the pivot man.

Option 1 (Diagram 8-40): The guard G-1 can pass the ball into the forward and then cut on either side. (The other guard then may break into the spot which was vacated by the passing guard.)

Option 2 (Diagram 8-41): The guard can pass in to the forward and then screen for the other guard G-2. The forward can pass in to the pivot and cut or screen.

Option 3 (Diagram 8-42): The guard G-1 can pass the ball in to the pivot and then screen for the other guard G-2. If G-2 is not open he can screen for the pivot man or for the forward.

Option 4 (Diagram 8-43): The guard G-2 can pass to G-1 and then screen for the forward F-2. G-1 can then pass to F-2.

Option 5 (Diagram 8-44): On Option 4, if the pass cannot go in to F-2, then the guard G-2 can block out F-2 and screen for F-1. G-1 can then pass in to F-1.

Five-man plays

After operating a four-man offense for some time, then you may move on to the full five-man offensive pattern. All players should be able to play in more than one position. The pivot man should be able to play in both pivot or forward positions. The guards should be able to play both guard or forward spots, and the forwards should be able to play the pivot or even a guard spot, if necessary.

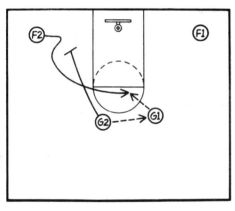

Diagram 8-43

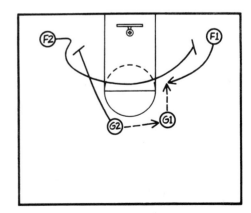

Diagram 8-44

With five men you can start with any of the two-man plays, which may then involve a third, fourth, or fifth player. The play can then become perpetual by having a definite rotation pattern set up (see Chapter 9). You should always have at least one guard out court, ready to fall back on defense. You should always have balance inside so that you have good rebounding position.

With the five-man plays you can use all of the two-, three-, and four-man options, plus the involvement of the fifth man.

Option 1 (Diagram 8-45): The pivot man can screen for the weak-side forward as a guard-guard or a guard-forward play is started.

Option 2 (Diagram 8-46): If the guards are having difficulty getting the inside pass in, then the forwards can change positions on the floor.

Option 3 (Diagram 8-47): The ball can go in to one forward and then the pivot man can screen the weak-side forward. The guard can screen the weak-side guard.

Option 4 (Diagram 8-48): The ball can go into the pivot and the guards can cross out court, as both forwards break for the goal for a possible pass. If the shot is not taken by the pivot man or passed back out to a guard, the forwards can come out on the side opposite that which they started on (maintaining floor balance).

Option 5 (Diagram 8-49): The ball can go in to the pivot from the guard G-2. The pivot can pass and screen for F-1 as G-2 goes down to screen for F-2.

Keep it simple—learn to use your plays

This offense may seem complicated, but it is really very simple. It utilizes all of the basic offensive fundamentals of pass and cut,

Diagram 8-45	*Diagram 8-46*

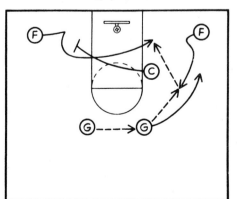 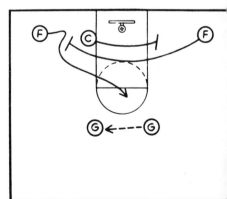

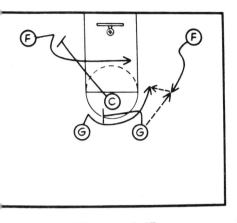

Diagram 8-47

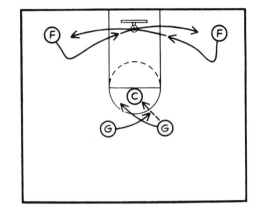

Diagram 8-48

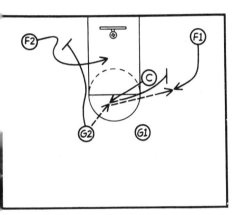

Diagram 8-49

pass and screen, and screen and roll. There are no signals for the plays and the options do not go by any number. The players must learn to use the various options according to the way that the defense is playing them.

Keep your offense simple and basic. Do not have a lot of numbered plays which if stopped keep the offense from moving. A moving offense is a must in order to create scoring opportunities. Learn the basic plays and always have another option ready to materialize if the first move fails. There are many other options other than those shown which can be developed and added to the offense as the season progresses. *Fit the pattern to the material, rather than the material to the pattern.*

Take into consideration individual skills and potential in developing the proper patterns for your particular team. Options which are successful with one group of players may be a complete failure with the following year's team.

Consider the speed of your guards, their ball-handling and passing skill, their ability to shoot set shots, and their ability to shoot on the move. Consider the best moves of your pivot man and whether he can go both right and left. Know your forwards well, and understand their individual strengths and weaknesses. Where can each player seem to play best? What are his favorite shooting spots? What are his best moves? Can he score well with one-on-one situations? Does he need screens to get his shot? Does a player have obvious weaknesses which can be detected by the opposition? Can he get his shot against a good defensive man? Does a player look good in practice or without opposition, but tighten up against a real opponent? Does each player seem to be contributing his best for the good of the entire team? Do certain players seem to be able to work better together than with others? Is the pattern getting the most out of the players?

These are just a few of the questions which the coach must ask himself in making his offensive plans. He should sit down and take a good over-all look at the team from the standpoint of an opposing coach. He should ask, "How would I try to defense this team?"

After all of these considerations, then the coach is in a better position to fit his patterns to his material. The coach is also more enlightened concerning the weakness of his squad and can better devise remedial practice programs for the team and for individuals.

9

The Perpetual-Pattern
Man-to-Man Offense

The perpetual-pattern offense is a constantly moving offense. It puts together individual moves, two-man plays, three-man plays, four-man plays, and five-man plays. The players should never run out of options which may be used to find openings in the defense. If one play does not produce a good scoring opportunity, the next one may. If the play does not work on one side of the floor, it may work on the other side. One screen or cut may produce an opening at one time, but several screens or cuts may be necessary to get a good shot at some other time.

The perpetual pattern must be used with speed, patience, skill, and finesse. The individual players must know their own abilities and must learn to pick the first good opening in the defense. Don't waste a shot or possible loss of the ball unless you are able to get a better than 50-50 chance at scoring. Play the percentages, but don't pass up any quick openings. Put the pressure on the defense.

The old saying "All things come to him who waits" is not true in basketball! It should say "All things come to him who *works*."

After several poor shots are taken, some coaches and players will cry "Slow down your offense." *Never* slow down your offense. You may work the ball longer before shooting, but if you really slow down your offense, you are just co-operating with the defensive team. A slowed down offense is the easiest offense to stop. A patient, aggressive, moving, pressure-type offense is the hardest to defend against. The perpetual-pattern team never runs out of patience nor plays.

Perpetual-pattern man-to-man offensive principles

Against a man-to-man defense the perpetual-pattern offense attempts to capitilize on individual fundamentals in one-on-one situations. It uses cuts, pull-outs, screens, and rolls in order to counteract the team man-to-man defense.

The first responsibility for making a play on offense is upon the man with the ball. The man who makes the pass must then make the play. As he passes the ball there are three basic things that he may do: 1) *cut* toward the pass receiver or toward the goal, 2) *screen* for the pass receiver or for a man who does not have the ball, 3) *pass* and then *hold-up*, as a signal for the pass receiver or another player to set the screen for him.

The second responsibility for making the offense move is upon the nearest logical pass receivers. If the man with the ball is having difficulty in making the pass, then the logical pass receivers must either: 1) *cut* toward the man with the ball or fake and reverse toward the goal, 2) *change positions* with another offensive man, 3) *pull out* by moving out of the way of the man with the ball and giving him room to operate against his man in a one-on-one situation, or 4) set a *screen* for the man with the ball or for another player who does not have the ball.

The third responsibility for the movement of the offense is upon the weak-side players. The weak-side men can help a bogged-down offense by 1) *cutting* across the court into position to receive a pass, or 2) by setting a *screen* for the man who does not have the ball to roll around and receive a pass.

Importance of floor balance

No matter what offensive plan you use, you must have players who know their positions and how to play them. The pattern must have balance and continuity. The positions on the floor should not become bunched up or crowded. If two players are close together this bunches the defense and makes it much harder to penetrate with the offense. In order to maintain floor balance, players should be able to play for short periods in any floor position necessary. There should be a constant movement of men and the ball into different areas of the floor, but never a stoppage or clogging of the normal flow of the offensive pattern.

Basic perpetual patterns

There are three basic floor patterns which we use with our man-to-man offense. They are the two-one-two pattern, the one-three-one pattern, and the three-two pattern. The man-to-man principles apply no matter which pattern is being used. The basic options which were discussed in Chapter 8 may be used with all three of the patterns. The basic continuity is the same with each. Special plays for each of the patterns may be developed later in the year, after basic options are well developed and are used with skill. Floor balance and rebounding position are important to all three patterns, for offensive as well as defensive purposes.

The two-one-two

The basic two-one-two set up is with two guards out front, a pivot man working the key area, and two forwards. The forwards set up on each side of the floor, about six feet from the side line and about the same distance from the base line (Diagram 9-1).

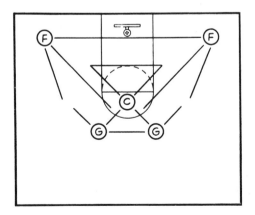

Diagram 9-1

Rotation on the two-one-two

Any of the options discussed in Chapter 8 may be used with the two-one-two. Floor balance and movement may be maintained by several different rotation methods. Any time that one guard passes the ball and leaves this area, the other guard should be ready to break into the position which was vacated. Only one guard should be allowed to move in past the foul line at any one time. The back guard is for defensive purposes and also for purposes of having a safety valve or outlet if the play is not successful. Having a man back to pass the ball to insures having someone to pass to at all times and helps to keep the plays in constant action. (Diagram 9-2).

If G-1 goes in and G-2 assumes his position, the ball is passed back to G-2. Then G-1 can come back out on the other side of the floor and into G-2's original position (Diagram 9-3).

If G-1 cannot get back into G-2's original position very quickly after the pass out to G-2, then F-2 can assume that position and G-1 can take F-1's position for a play or so (Diagram 9-4).

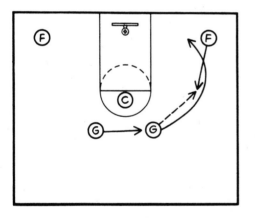

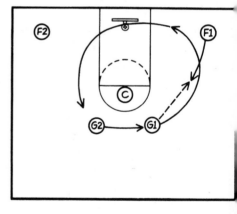

Diagram 9-2   **Diagram 9-3**

On this offense the three inside men can exchange positions at any time (Diagram 9-5). The guards try to maintain their positions as much as possible but can play an inside position for short periods. One guard should be back at all times.

If the play is started on one side of the floor and is not successful, the ball can be passed back out to the other guard. The weak-

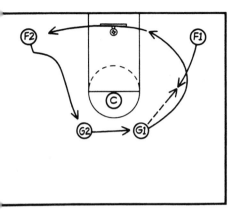

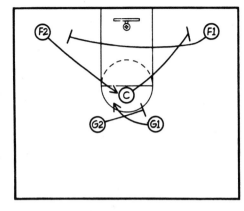

Diagram 9-4   **Diagram 9-5**

side forward can come out into the other guard spot. The guard cutting through can take the forward spot and start a play on the opposite side of the floor. G-1 passes to F-1 and cuts on the outside. G-2 breaks into G-1's old position. The ball is passed back out to G-2. F-2 breaks out into G-2's original spot and G-2 passes the ball to him (F-2). G-1 breaks into F-2's original spot. F-2 and G-1 can then continue play (Diagram 9-6).

If the ball goes in to the center and one guard cuts through or goes inside to screen, the other guard can assume his position (Diagram 9-7).

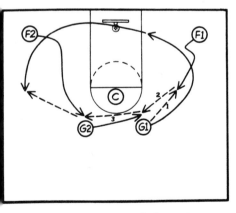

Diagram 9-7

Diagram 9-6

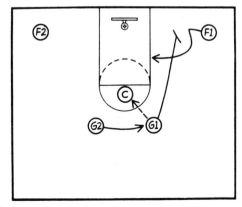

The forward can screen for a guard on the weak side and then assume his position on the floor for a play or so. G-2 passes in to C and then screens for F-2. F-1, who is on the weak side, breaks for the goal down the weak side of the floor. F-1 must be sure to assume G-1's guard position. If the play does not work, you will have a man out court to pass the ball to and keep the action going (Diagram 9-8).

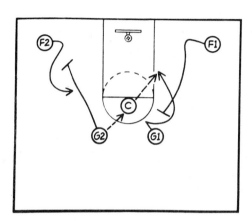

Diagram 9-8

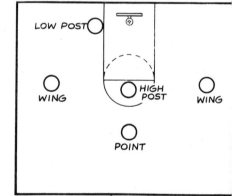

Diagram 9-9

The one-three-one pattern

The one-three-one pattern uses a point man out court, a low post man back under the goal, a high post man in the middle at the foul line, and two wing men on the sides (Diagram 9-9).

ROTATION ON THE ONE-THREE-ONE

The basic one-on-one maneuvers, two-man plays, three-man plays, four-man plays, and five-man plays described in Chapter 8 may be used with this pattern.

The principles of rotation, balance, pass-and-cut, pass-and-screen, and screen-and-roll which were used in the two-one-two are used with the one-three-one offense. You are simply learning to use the same principles with a different basic floor arrangement.

The wing men are very often in position to use one-on-one maneuvers and your best offensive players should play these positions. The point man should be a good ball-handler and playmaker. The low post man should be a good rebounder and be able to score close in. The high post should be a good pivot man with good feed-off ability.

Basically, the wing men and point men should be able to interchange positions and the two post men should be able to pick and roll for each other at any time. The three out-court men (two wing men and the point man) can run a three-man weave and the two inside men (the low and high post) can run a two-man roll (Diagram 9-10).

If W-1 goes in for the goal, then P can assume the wing man's position on that side. W-2 can break up to the point position. W-1 can then come back out to the other wing position. H and L can change positions at any time (Diagram 9-11).

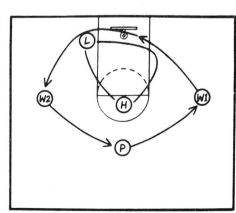

Diagram 9-11

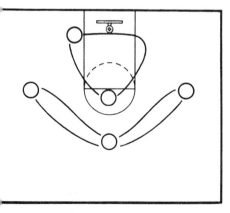

Diagram 9-10

The post men should be able to screen for the wing men and assume their positions for a short time (Diagrams 9-12 and 9-13).

Rebounding from the One-Three-One

It is important to keep the offense balanced and moving at all times. A point man should always be back for outlet passes and for defense. The post men should be ready to move in on the boards at any time. The weak-side wing man can go in for the rebound and the other wing man can play the high bounding rebound and be ready to fall back on defense (Diagram 9-14).

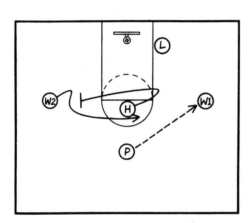

Diagram 9-12

Diagram 9-13

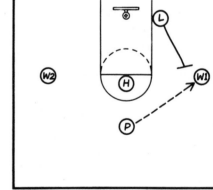

The three-two pattern

The three-two pattern is used against a very tight man-to-man defense. It is very good against a tall team because it can help pull the big men away from the goal. The basic pattern is with three men out court and the two post men in the corners. The offense tries to pull out the defense and keep the center open. The offense plays out as far as the defense will come and get them (Diagram 9-15).

PLAYS WITH THE THREE-TWO

The basic one-on-one maneuvers, and two-, three-, four-, and five-man plays with the two-one-two and the one-three-one are

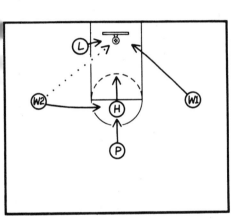

Diagram 9-14

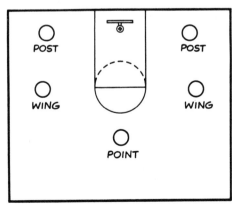

Diagram 9-15

used. The same principles of rotation and pass, cut, screen, and roll are used with the three-two. The responsibilities for making action and plays are the same on all three of these basic patterns (Diagrams 9-16, 9-17, 9-18, 9-19).

ROTATION ON THE THREE-TWO

The rotation is similar to the one-three-one rotation. The three out-court men can exchange positions at any time and the two deep post men can screen and exchange positions (Diagram 9-20).

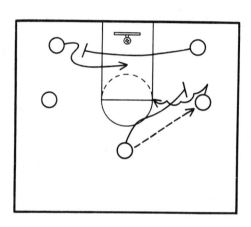

Diagram 9-16

Diagram 9-17

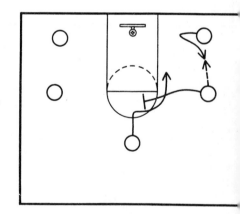

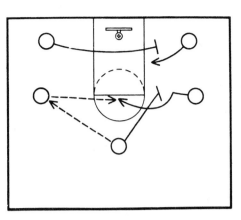

Diagram 9-18

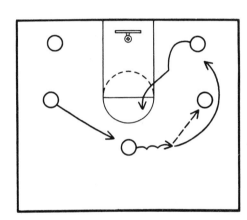

Diagram 9-19

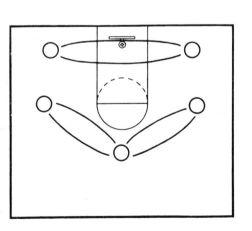

Diagram 9-20

115

The post men can screen for the wing men and assume their positions at times. The wing men can screen for the post men and then assume their places (Diagram 9-21).

Quick opening high post plays may be executed. If the pass does not go into the key, the post man should clear out, in order to keep the middle open for driving and cutting (Diagram 9-22).

REBOUNDING FROM THE THREE-TWO

The three-two should pull the big men away from the goal and give the offense a good opportunity to move in on the boards. The post men always move in for rebound position. If the shot is taken from the left-hand side, then the right wing man can move in on the goal. The point man is ready to go back on defense with the left wing man. If the shot is taken on the other side the reverse is true (Diagram 9-23).

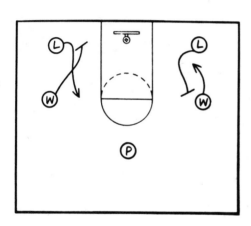

Diagram 9-21

Diagram 9-22

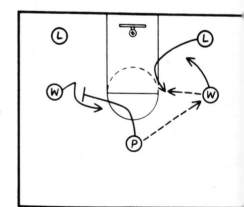

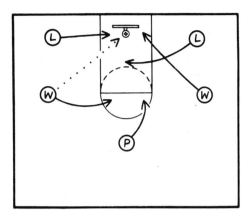

Diagram 9-23

Adapting the patterns to your material

The ability of your players to run each of the three basic patterns may vary. Their size, speed, shooting ability, and ball-handling skill will determine to a large extent, which patterns you will use most. The way the other team defenses you will also be one of the deciding factors.

If your players are pretty much the same size you may use a different rotation system than you would if you had one or two very tall players. You may want to keep a rebound expert in good rebounding position, or a good side-shooter in his favorite position. The rotation scheme may usually be altered to accommodate some of these special cases with the perpetual-pattern offense.

Many pet plays and individual moves may be developed with the step-by-step procedure described in Chapter 8. Your offense should be so well developed that you could show your plays to the opposition and still be able to score against them.

10

The Perpetual-Pattern
Zone Offense

The perpetual-pattern zone offense may use the same three basic floor patterns as the man-to-man. The difference is in the rotation and the use of the zone offensive fundamentals. With the perpetual-pattern zone offense there are also different options and moves which may be made. The play is balanced and has definite continuity, just as does the man-to-man. The fast-break attempt is one good weapon to use against a zone defense. If the fast-break attempt is stopped the perpetual-pattern zone offense should go into immediate action. The play should be patient, but not slow. Again as with the man-to-man, the more offensive moves that are made, the more the number of defensive moves and shifts which are required. Eventually defensive errors will be committed which lead to openings. The shot may be taken in a few seconds or after one or two minutes, depending upon offensive openings. Don't wait for the good shot—create it!

The perpetual-pattern zone-offensive principles

In the attack against a zone defense a team must take a good look at what the defense is attempting to do. Remember that a zone defense points toward the man who has the ball, and may lose contact with some of the other offensive players. Many teams become "frozen" against a zone defense and try to beat them by only passing the ball. If the opposition blocks the passing lanes they are in trouble. A good zone offense must move not only the ball but also men.

The zone defense attempts to cover men in certain areas. If a man stands in one area he is very easy for the defensive man to cover. If he moves from one area to another the defense is forced to make changes. It is when they are shifting and making these area changes that defensive errors are committed.

There are several good offensive principles which can be used effectively against a zone defense. The perpetual-pattern offense attempts to incorporate all of these principles into their attack. (1) One is the use of the *fast break*. Always force the zone to get back fast or else take the quick advantage by outnumbering them at the offensive end of the floor. (2) *Pass the ball* rapidly and with deception. Forcing the defense to shift with every pass, may force them to become over-committed. If the defense allows you to pass the ball freely, then do so and try to get the defense over-shifted. (3) If the defense covers the passing lanes, then *move men*. It will be difficult for them to cover both the passing lanes and men moving from one area to another. (4) Another principle is *over-loading* some of the areas, putting two men in an area covered by only one man. You may use the over-load and the over-shifting principles together on a rotation from one side of the floor to another. (5) *Split the defense*. Put one offensive man in between two defensive men and keep them tied up on their defensive commitments. (6) *Screen* the zone. Don't be afraid to try screens in certain situations from time to time against a zone. A normal screening offense will not be too effective, but side men out court can often be screened off and prevented from shifting properly. The resulting two-on-one situation on the side of the court then can be capitalized on. The man who sets the outside screen will have rolling or inside position on the man that he screens. (7) Don't be afraid to attempt a *drive* against a zone, if you get in a one-on-one situation. If they do send another man to help stop the drive, then you may be able to feed the ball in under to the man that the defense left in order to cover you.

Make sure that they zone-defense you

Some teams will alternate their defenses and run a zone defense one time that they come down the floor and switch to a man-to-man the next time. They may have keys to switching their defense. For example they may use a two-one-two zone after a scored free-throw, a three-two zone after a violation, a man-to-man after a scored field goal, and so on. You must be ready to alter your offensive attack accordingly.

If they match you up on defense, try man-to-man principles

Some teams will go into a zone defense in order to force a team to stop the movement of their offense. Once they have stopped your movement they will match up man-to-man on the men in their area. This makes their defensive job much simpler. Keep the defense honest by constantly testing them. Try your man-to-man offensive principles from time to time. Don't assume that the zone defense will stop all drives and all screens and rolls—make them prove it. You will be surprised how often they will work. If they do not work, you go right ahead uninterrupted with your zone attack. This is another great advantage of the perpetual-pattern offense.

The two-one-two pattern

The basic two-one-two placement of men is the same as the two-one-two man-to-man offense. The two guards should be the best ball-handlers and play-makers. The forwards should be able to move well and shoot from the sides or corners; the tallest or best rebounder can play in the pivot position. The players should not feel restricted to their spots, and should move both within their own areas and also between areas from time to time (Diagram 10-1).

The players should move to meet the pass in their area. Do not stand and wait for the ball. Pass the ball rapidly and deceptively to get the defense over-shifted. The forwards should move in

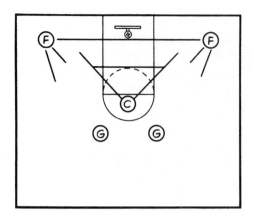

Diagram 10-1

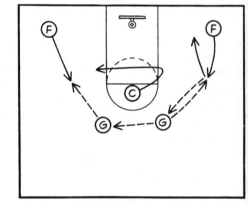

Diagram 10-2

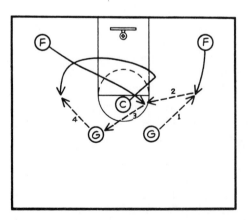

Diagram 10-3

piston-like action, coming up to meet the pass on the ball side and going back down to the base line on the weak side. The pivot man should also move and make the defense work to cover him (Diagram 10-2).

The inside men can exchange areas at any time. The pivot man can move out to a side area and a forward can take the pivot position for awhile. If the defense does not challenge the passing lanes, you should be able to get good shots after a few passes (Diagram 10-3).

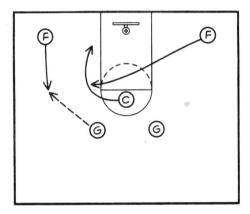

Diagram 10-4

Rotation on the two-one-two zone offense

Movement of men inside the zone can begin at any time that the defense starts to contest the passing lanes. If the ball is passed in to a forward, the pivot man should roll for the bucket. His roll can serve two purposes: 1) he may get into position to receive a pass, or 2) he can pull the defense in toward the goal. As soon as the pivot man leaves his area, then the weak-side forward can break into the lane for a possible opening. If the pivot man did not get open he goes on out to the forward area and the forward becomes the pivot man (Diagram 10-4).

If the pivot man or forward did not get a good shot, then he can pass the ball rapidly back out to a guard, who can continue play. The rotation can be run on the opposite side of the floor and so on. The rotation can continue with the man in the pivot rolling with a pass into the side and the weak-side forward breaking in to assume the pivot spot (Diagram 10-5).

When the ball is passed into the pivot position by a guard, a different rotation system may be initiated. You can produce an overload by having the forward on the side of the pass (F-1) break up to the foul line, and the other forward (F-2) break into his original area (Diagram 10-6).

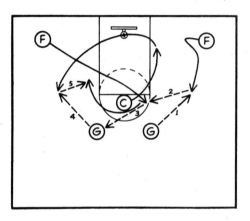

Diagram 10-5

Diagram 10-6

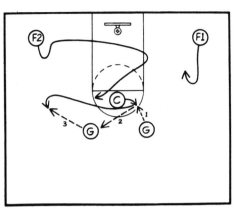

Diagram 10-7

Diagram 10-8

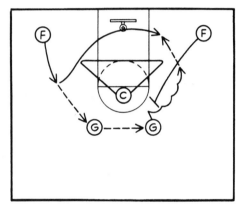

If F-1 or F-2 were not open on the above rotation, the pivot man can fire the ball back out to the side and F-2 can break into his vacated spot and middle rotation may continue again as in Diagram 10-5 (Diagram 10-7).

Screening of the zone can work when a forward comes up to screen for a guard as he receives a quick pass. The forward on the weak side may cut across the lane. If the guard is stopped as he comes around the screen, he may feed under (Diagram 10-8).

The guards may rotate by cutting down the weak side on the

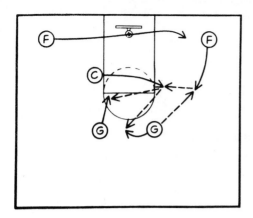

Diagram 10-9

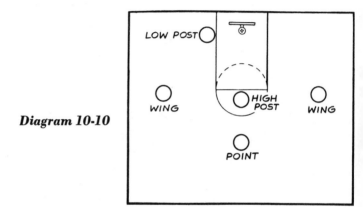

Diagram 10-10

over-load. The other guard should assume the cutter's position, if the ball is passed to C (Diagram 10-9).

The one-three-one pattern

The placement of men in the one-three-one zone is the same as with the man-to-man. There are a point man, two wing men, a high post man, and a low post man. This is the basic placement, but the men must feel free to roam some within their area and must break up to meet passes (Diagram 10-10).

Movement from various areas can also be used, with the high and low post men exchanging positions at any time. The wing men can also exchange areas with one wing man going to the corner and the other wing man coming across the key area (Diagram 10-11).

Rotation on the one-three-one zone offense

Movement of men can be accomplished with continuity. When the ball is passed to a wing man (W-1), the low post man (L) can break out to the corner on that side of the floor. If the wing man (W-1) passes to the low post man (L), then he cuts through toward the goal. The point man (P) can break into the wing position for a possible return pass. The other wing man (W-2) breaks into the point position for a possible quick pass. If W-1 does not get the ball, or if there is no shot taken, he may come out on the other side of the floor into W-2's original position and play continues. If the pass is to W-2, then the play is the same but on the other side of the floor (Diagram 10-12).

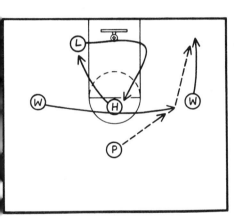

Diagram 10-11

Diagram 10-12

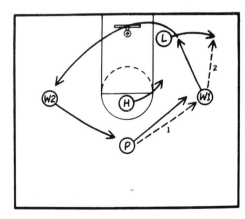

If the pass is made in to the high pivot man (H) then an over-load situation can be brought about by the movements of the low post man (L) to the corner on his side of the floor and the opposite wing man (W-2) into the low post position. The high post man fires the ball to W-1 or any open man (Diagram 10-13).

If a good shot did not result from the overload the ball can be passed back out to the point man (P). W-2 can break back into the wing position and the low post man (L) can come back across the key area. The point man can fire the ball over to the weak side for a possible open shot by W-2 or L on the shift (Diagram 10-14).

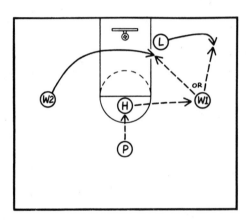

Diagram 10-13

Diagram 10-14

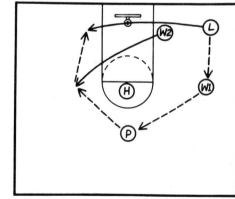

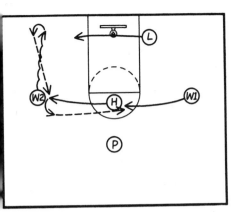

Diagram 10-15

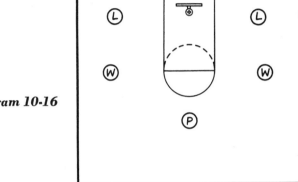

Diagram 10-16

If the wing man (W-2) has the ball and decides to drive he can go for the base line and a different type of rotation will be called for. The high post man (H) can break into the wing position, the low post man (L) can break across the key, and the other wing man (W-1) can break into the high post position (Diagram 10-15).

The three-two zone-offense pattern

The perpetual-pattern zone offense can also be run out of the three-two setup. If you are running out of the three-two man-to-man offense and the other team starts to zone you on defense, you needn't stop to change your whole offensive setup. You only have to change the plan for attacking their defense. This basic three-men-out, two-in offense is in very good position to move the ball rapidly around the outside of the zone and can break quickly into the middle area to penetrate the zone (Diagram 10-16).

If you have trouble moving the ball around the outside, then you can start moving men inside the zone. One of the deep post men can break into the key area at any time. If the defense collapses on him, then he can feed the ball out to any open man (Diagram 10-17).

The overload may be accomplished by one of the deep post men breaking across the floor from the weak side and a man from the weak side and a man from the weak-side wing position breaking into the high post. The ball can be fed into the man who is open (Diagram 10-18).

If no opening occurred in the overload, it can be swung to the other side of the floor by these men reversing back to their

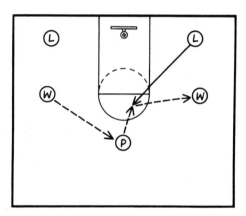

Diagram 10-17

Diagram 10-18

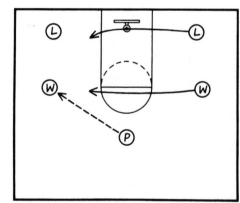

original positions. The deep post man and wing man can then cross the floor to over-load on the opposite side of the floor. This may be reversed back and forth several times if necessary (Diagram 10-19).

Rotation from the three-two zone offense

If the ball is passed by the point man (P) to a side man (W-1), the point man can cut down the middle to pull the defense in. The other side man (W-2) can break into the point position for a pass. The weak-side deep post man can break into W-2's position and the point man can break into the deep post position. If the pass is to W-2 the rotation is the opposite (Diagram 10-20).

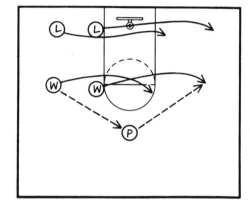

Diagram 10-19

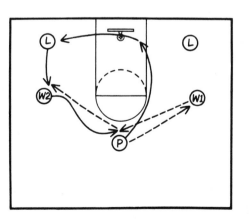

Diagram 10-20

If the ball is passed to a deep post man by W-2, then he can cut for the basket to pull the defense in for the point man (P) who breaks into W-2's position for a quick pass, as the weak-side deep post man takes W-1's position. The ball can then be passed into W-2, who is breaking out on the weak side of the floor. If this does not produce a good shot, balance can be resumed and play can continue (Diagram 10-21).

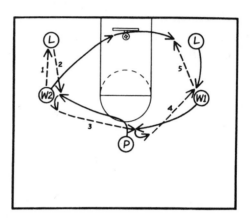

Diagram 10-21

Adjusting the zone pattern to your player personnel

The perpetual-pattern zone offense should be patterned to fit your personnel. Do not plan to use the same rotation, inside movement, or overload one year to the next. You must know the capabilities of all of your players and you must adjust the patterns to take full advantage of their strengths and minimize their weaknesses.

The zone-offensive team must have confidence in themselves and in their offensive patterns. The patterns must be operated as a team. Proper preparation against all types of zone defenses can insure confidence, avoid excitement, and keep you from falling into the hands of the zone defense.

The important tactic against the zone defense is to keep the offense moving. Your individual adjustments must not stop or slow down the play of the team. Continuity must be maintained.

If one play does not develop, you must be able to move right on into another option. The patterns must be practiced until they are habit. The players should have a good idea of what may or may not work well against all types of zone defenses. All of the zone offensive principles must be incorporated into the basic zone patterns in order to insure their proper utilization.

11

Developing the Triple-A
Defense

*(Aggressive Man-to-Man,
Alternating Zone, and
Aggravating Press Defense)*

We believe that defense is one of
the most neglected phases of the game of basketball. This part
of the game goes unappreciated by many fans, sports writers,
players, and coaches. Many people give defense lip service, but
talk is cheap. Just as the squeaking wheel is the one that gets the
grease, the offensive star is the man who gets the praise.

Many coaches will say, "I am a great believer in sound defense," and spend hours and hours working on plays, patterns, and
other offensive parts of the game. They spend only minutes
working on defense. They believe that defense is really an individual thing and that it will somehow take care of itself. They
feel an urgency for team organization on offense but lack this
strong feeling concerning defensive play.

Defense is a team affair

Defense is no more of an individual matter than offense. It is just as urgent to have good organization on defense. Defensive strategy must be just as well prepared as offensive strategy. Defense requires time, patience, and hard work. All of this must be planned for in the practice schedule and time must be allotted for this important work. Every man on the team must be sold on the value of team defense. He must know his job and be able to do it well. He must feel just as bad if he has a poor defensive night as if he has a low scoring game. The value of teamwork on defense cannot be overly stressed or emphasized.

Defense is hard work

Many people seem to have the opinion that good defense must go hand in hand with slow, deliberate offense. They believe that a low-scoring basketball game indicates good defense. This is not necessarily true in basketball, because each time you score the other team will get possession of the ball. The more times you score, the more times your opponents will have an opportunity to score also. The most important thing is the difference between the number of times that you score and the number of times that you prevent the opposition from scoring.

We feel that much of the success of our basketball teams in the past has been due to sound, aggressive defensive play as well as aggressive offense. The year that our squad averaged over 117.0 points in conference play and set a new NJCAA National Tournament scoring record we had one of the best defensive squads that I have ever coached. Much of our scoring was due to an untiring, hard-working, aggressive defense. We obtained possession of the ball many times by making steals and making the other team force shots, commit wild passes and travel violations, and so forth. We averaged nearly 100 shots per game. You could not possibly play a poor defense and still gain possession of the ball that many times. Most of these shots were good percentage shots also, as we averaged hitting 48 per cent of our field goal attempts.

Defense requires enthusiasm

Hustle wins ball games. This hustle does not apply to just one end of the court. Resting while on defense is inexcusable. A player who only wants to work on offense is hurting the team. It is possible to work hard on offense and still carry this enthusiasm over into defensive play. In fact, we find that if a squad really starts to hustle at one end of the court, this hustle usually is carried over to the other end of the floor. In order for a team to play in this manner, they must have the proper attitude and motivation and be in top physical condition.

The philosophy of the Triple-A defense

Many teams believe in a varied offensive attack, according to the opponent, their personnel, their defense, the game situation, and the talents of their own players; but they play defense only one way. They try to play defense the same way year after year, no matter what their individual personnel is like from one year to the next. We believe that defense must be just as well planned and patterned for individual players as offense.

The Triple-A defense is a method of defense which utilizes all three defensive styles of play. It involves being able to change defenses as the need arises. A versatile defensive team is not surprised by any offensive strategy. The Triple-A defensive idea includes an aggressive man-to-man defense, an alternating zone defense, and an aggravating press defense. The Triple-A defense is ready for any opponent or any game situation which may arise.

Developing the Triple-A defense

The Triple-A defense is a versatile defensive plan. It is not easy to teach. It must be taught patiently, step by step. It must be developed slowly in units as the players show a readiness and desire to learn and use more defensive strategy.

The Triple-A defensive plan is a long-term investment. It may take the entire season or longer to develop. In high school it may be spread and developed over a two- or three-year period. Like many long-term investments, a versatile defense is sound and will pay good dividends in the end.

Build slow but build solid

Do not try to teach players two or three defensive styles at the same time. They will become confused and will not really learn to use any of them well. They may become "jacks of all trades and masters of none." We attempt to master the defenses one at a time. Finally we are able to put them all together for a three-pronged defense. The defense, like the offense, must be built bit by bit upon a solid foundation.

Man-to-man defense first

In the development of the Triple-A idea, we always start with the basic man-to-man defense. As the players become proficient in basic man-to-man defense, we then add the aggressive style of man-to-man. The time spent on the man-to-man styles will vary with individual personnel from a few weeks to half of the season. After they have mastered this phase we move on to the zone defense.

Zone defense

We feel that a good zone defense is only as strong as the individuals who are working it. The zone defense should not be thought of as a last resort defense or a miracle defense. The zone defense is only one weapon which may be used against the enemy. It can be a very valuable weapon, if it is developed fully. The zone defense ideas and principles must be fully explained and understood by all. The players must understand, what they are trying to do, how, and why.

Press defense

After the players are capable of utilizing both the aggressive man-to-man and the alternating zone defenses we move into the third phase of the Triple-A defensive plan. This phase is the aggravating press defense.

The aggravating press defense utilizes both the man-to-man and zone defensive principles. We have a zone press phase, a man-to-man press phase, and a combination zone and man-to-man phase. The players must have good man-to-man fundamentals and sound zone defensive skills. The press style of play cannot be successful without these two ingredients, and a third, which is hustle or desire.

Practice all phases of the Triple-A defense

After the basic principles of this three-pronged defensive plan are learned, all phases must be constantly revised and polished. Prime practice time must be allotted for defense. It should not be just something that you do if you have time. You must find time for defense. It is very easy to "unlearn" things which are not used every day. If you find that you are using one part of the Triple-A more than some other phase, you must constantly brush up on the unused phases. You may begin to find that teams are starting to point at this one phase of your defense.

The importance of individual defensive fundamentals

"A chain is only as strong as its weakest link." Smart teams will look for individual weaknesses and try to exploit them. Time spent on individual defensive fundamentals is time well spent. Just as with offense, a good defense is the putting together of five outstanding individuals with a common goal in mind. One weak player can spoil the plans and efforts of the other four men. Without individual fundamentals there can be no purposeful organized team defensive strategy.

Some coaches believe that a zone defense will cover up for weak defensive players. Others think that a sagging man-to-man can help cover up for a weak defensive man. Any way you look at it, a weak defensive man interferes with your defensive strategy and is hurting your team play. The only way to cure this weakness is to teach defensive fundamentals or look for new personnel. You must ask yourself if this player is really contributing enough to the team effort. We believe that if a player possesses the necessary physical attributes for being an offensive star, he also has the physical ability to play good sound defense. Often a lack is just a matter of motivation and emphasis. A player must understand that even though he is scoring quite a number of points he is still hurting the team if he loafs or is not able to play full-time defense. Defensive ability is not inherited, it is acquired. Acquired characteristics come from the environment: it is up to the coach to set up the proper environment for acquiring defensive skills.

Using your defense to full advantage

The Triple-A defensive idea attempts to take full advantage of all of your players' individual defensive skills. In addition to this, it gives you a choice of weapons which may be employed according to the game situation, your opponent's material, and the style of play or strategy employed by your opponent. For example your players may be able to employ one phase of defense, such as the aggressive man-to-man, very effectively. If an opponent points his offense at this type of defense, a switch to a good zone defense may confuse his plans. The opponent may have spent days working his offense against the defense that he thought you would employ. The time that he spent on this was time that he was not working on his own defense. The element of surprise is an element which should not be overlooked in your defensive strategy.

If you have a tall, slow group of players you may want to rely mostly on a zone or sagging defense. This would help your players near the goal in order to take advantage of your height. If you are small and fast you may want to play aggressive man-to-man or pressing go-get-'em ball to take advantage of your speed. No matter which principle of style you employ, you should still have more than one defense in your bag of tricks. You should not find yourself in a position where you are forced to play the other team's style of ball game. Being able to effectively use more than one kind of offense and defense, helps to put you in a better position, in order to control the style and pace of the ball game.

A winning team uses its material to best advantage

Your player personnel may vary from year to year. The size and speed of your players may dictate the principle style of defense which you may employ. However, other methods of defense may be effective for short periods of time or in certain game situations. If you have not developed other types of defense during the year, you cannot suddenly decide to try something new at tournament time or when you are behind in scoring.

Every team should have a firsthand working knowledge of man-to-man, zone, and pressing defenses. When, where, and how much each of these defenses is used depends of course upon your individual players.

With a lot of time, patience, and work you may be surprised how versatile almost any basketball team may become on defense. A versatile defense is like safety belts in your automobile. You may not need them all the time, but the one time that you do need them they are very worthwhile, and if you don't use them all the time you are not prepared for the time that you do need them.

Take time for defense

The coach who says, "I don't have time to teach defense," will have plenty of time on his hands next March. At tournament time, the season ends very quickly for the poor defensive team. The team that is not prepared to stop many types of offensive attacks will fall by the wayside early.

The Triple-A idea—be prepared

The real value of the Triple-A defense does not appear early in the season, but comes to the fore in its readiness to play any kind of defense that is needed when the chips are down. The Triple-A is a well-planned, co-ordinated, balanced plan of defensive play.

The aggressive man-to-man phase is ready to upset and throw off balance any man-to-man attack. This defense does not sit back and wait for the offense to make their plays. It is designed to interfere with the way that the other team wants to play. It anticipates plays and stops them before they start. It is patient but not retiring. It is aggressive, but not overanxious. It is basically man-to-man, but it is not every man for himself. It is a five-man team defense, but each man must know and do his job.

The alternating zone defensive phase of the Triple-A is ready to stop any man-to-man or zone attack. It is designed to get the most out of the defensive material that you have available. It is a team defense, but requires good individual fundamentals. It is not a sit-back-in-the-hole-and-wait-for-them-to-shoot defense. It is designed to confuse and bring to a halt a good, screening, well-moving offense. It is used to control the style and speed of the game. It gives the offense more to worry about and causes them to be disorganized in their offensive plans.

The aggravating press defensive phase of the Triple-A plan is your ace in the hole. The threat is always there. The offense is constantly worried about when and where it will strike. It may be used all during a game or only for special situations. It may be used to speed up the play of the game. It may be used to counteract a taller or slower team. It can be a surprise element. The aggravating press may be used to change certain defeat into glorious victory. It requires the best of fundamentals, conditioning, and desire. It is a daring defense, but it is designed to play the percentages. Learning to use it scientifically removes the elements of chance. The aggravating press can be highly aggravating to the opponent's plans for victory.

12

The Aggressive Man-to-Man Defense

I believe that a basketball player must know how to play man-to-man defense before he can play any other kind of defense. A group of weak defensive men using a zone defense will still be a weak defense. Various team defenses can help to cover up for individual mistakes, but each time they are forced to do so, it weakens the total defense. The fewer individual mistakes made, the stronger the team defense becomes. The greater the defensive base a team possesses, the more versatile and complex the total defensive strategy can become.

A player must learn to guard the man who has the ball. He must also be able to play effective defense against the man who does *not* have the ball. Some players want to work on defense only when their man has possession of the ball. They loaf or become observers when their man does not have the ball. This plays into the hands of a good offense.

Developing the aggressive man-to-man defense

Individual defense can be taught. We work very hard on one-on-one situations early in the season. Players are taught to guard the man with the ball, without any help from anyone else. Next we move on to two-on-two situations. Here they are taught to cover the man who does not have the ball as well. Sometimes the best way to defense a good player is not to let him get his hands on the ball in the first place. The next best way is not to let him have the ball in his favorite scoring position. You do not have a team defense if your players only play man-to-man defense when their man has possession of the ball. A five-man defense can beat a one-at-a-time defense any day of the week.

Build from the ground upward

After learning how to cover the man with and without the ball, then we move on to learning how and when to switch on defense. We go from the one-on-one and two-on-two situations to the three-on-three. We practice sliding through whenever we can. We switch only when we must. We learn to talk to each other on defense. Knowing what is going on around you on defense makes it much easier to know what you must do and when to do it.

After the three-on-three we involve a fourth player. We work on covering a man in the lane area who does not have the ball. We play in front of a man in the lane up to the high post position. We play the high post on the side. If a player cuts across the lane, we force him to cut behind the defensive man. We contest all passes into the scoring area. It is easier to cover a man in the scoring area before he has the ball than after he has it.

Finally we go to the five-on-five defense. We learn to switch back. When we get into mismatch situations we learn to call for help and to switch back from these situations at the earliest opportunity. We stress the full-time defensive idea and the element of a five-man team defense.

Types of man-to-man defenses

There are several ways in which the man-to-man defense can be played. One way is the tight man-to-man. Here each player is strictly responsible for his own man. Very little switching is used and it is every man for himself. This defense encourages individual aggressiveness and defensive skill, but does not develop too much in the way of the teamwork idea.

Another style of man-to-man defense is the free-switching man-to-man defense. Here switching is much more common and at times it may resemble a zone defense. Each player is responsible for a man, but he may not keep his original man for too long. The players may be matched up well at the start of this defense, but unless your team is well balanced in size, the mismatch situation will soon occur.

The third type is the sinking man-to-man defense. Here the players on the weak side will sag away from their man to the center of the floor or back toward the basket. This defense clogs the middle of the floor and makes passes into the pivot difficult; it may also help to stop drives toward the goal. This type of defense may be a little weak against good outside shooting. If the offense will move the ball rapidly from one side of the floor to the other, they may obtain good shots before the sagging men can get back out to cover them.

The basic principles of the aggressive man-to-man defense

The aggressive man-to-man defense is a combination of the tight man-to-man and the switching man-to-man defenses. It attempts to utilize the strong points of each of these defensive styles while at the same time minimizing all of their known weaknesses. The aggressive man-to-man is a vigorous full-time team defense.

The aggressive man-to-man attempts to use the ideas of individual aggressiveness and responsibility from the tight man-to-man defense, the ability to adjust to screens and defensive errors from the free switching man-to-man defense, and the ability to stop the drives and inside passes from the sagging man-to-man defense. All of these sound defensive ideas are incorporated into a single five-man team defense.

The known weakness of the three types of man-to-man defenses are minimized. The unfavorable screening position of the tight man-to-man is avoided. The idea of teamwork is stressed. The mismatch from the switch is quickly reversed and help is given to the defensive man in covering the unfavorable mismatch. The sagging man does not lose his man nor drop too far away from him. He must sag just enough to help out if he is needed to stop a drive or an inside passing threat. If he must cover a dangerous score situation he does so, since if he must leave his man his teammates are ready to help him out.

Stop the movement of the offense

Some man-to-man defenses mean keeping between your man and the basket at all times on defense. On the aggressive man-to-man we keep between our man and the basket *only* if he has the ball. We even violate this rule at times, if we are trying to lead a man where we want him to go. We may over-play to one side or the other to lead the dribbler into a trap or away from the scoring area. We take a part-way position against the players in the passing lanes. We not only attempt to cover the man, but we also anticipate and contest passes which may be made to him. We do not take foolish chances for pass interceptions. We don't really expect to intercept the ball each time, we are really only trying to force a slow-down in the movement of the offense. If you can slow down offensive action you are in a much better position to play effective team defense.

Force the cutter to go behind your back

If a man cuts toward the basket or out to receive a pass, the defense must anticipate his move and beat him there. He should be forced to go behind the defense. In making this move a player must watch for screens and get vocal advice and assistance from his teammates. Force the offense to attempt passes over the head of the defense. These are dangerous passes and will not pay off percentagewise for the offense. You will be able to deflect or pick off many of these passes. Do not gamble too much on this play, but make the offense think that you are over-playing the ball. Defensing the man without the ball can be just as much work as guarding the man who has the ball. In fact it may be more tiring at times.

Basic defensive positions on the aggressive man-to-man

One good advantage of the aggressive man-to-man is that you can match your players according to size, speed, agility, jumping ability, quickness, and general basketball know-how. The basic team alignment is with a tight man-to-man on the man with the ball. The man with the ball is the dangerous man at the moment.

We usually play him in a direct line between the ball and the basket, but we may over-play him slightly to one side or the other if we know which way he likes to go. We try to slow down and interfere with their normal pattern or style of play as much as possible.

The men who are in good cutting or pass-receiving position are the next most dangerous men at the moment. We attempt to anticipate their moves and beat them where they are going. We take up a part-way position against them, contesting all cuts and passes to these most logical pass receivers. The defensive man does not play in a direct line between his man and the basket, he will play part-way toward the ball. In this position he can cover the passing lane and he knows in which direction any cuts will occur.

We play in front of all men who are deep in the lane near the goal, between the man and the ball. Men who are about halfway along the lane will also be covered from the front or side. A man who is in the high post, near or on the foul line, will be covered from a side position. We contest all passes into this dangerous area, and try to cover the high post man on the side that the ball is on.

Men who are guarding players on the weak side sag toward the ball and into the middle of the court. The distance of the sag will vary with the distance of the offensive man to the ball. We play the man first and the ball second. A player is allowed to switch or leave his man only in emergency cases. The basic rule is to slow their offense down to a walk. It is much easier to play defense in slow motion.

The basic defensive positions against a two-one-two offense are shown in Diagrams 12-1 and 12-2.

The basic alignment against the one-three-one man-to-man attack utilizes the same basic principles of the aggressive man-to-man defense (Diagrams 12-3 and 12-4).

The basic defensive positions against the double post man-to-man attack are shown in Diagrams 12-5 and 12-6. We usually put our best rebounders against the post men, and our fastest men against the three outside men. We may switch a little more freely here, the two defensive post men with each other and the three outside men changing positions when necessary.

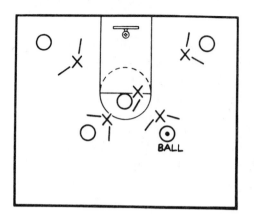

Diagram 12-1

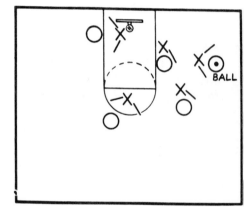

Diagram 12-2

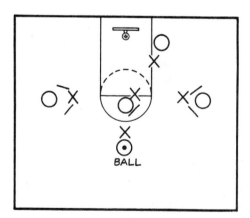

Diagram 12-3

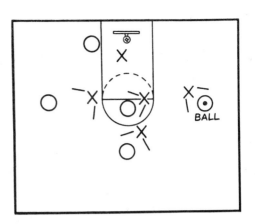

Diagram 12-4

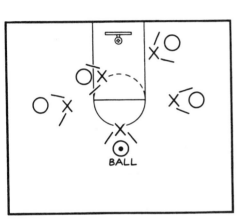

Diagram 12-5

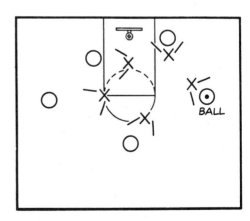

Diagram 12-6

149

Guarding the man with the ball

With the aggressive man-to-man defense, we play the man with the ball tight man-to-man. We give enough ground so that we are not easily faked out, but play close enough to avoid the quick jump shot. The defensive man covering the man with the ball assumes a good defensive position. The body is well balanced with the inside foot slightly forward, and the outside foot to the rear. The weight of the body is equal on both feet. The knees should be bent to give the body weight a good center of gravity. The inside hand should be extended in order to interfere with the shooter or to partially cover the potential passing lane. The outside hand should also be away from the body for balance and distraction.

The defensive player covering the man with the ball is between his man and the basket. He may vary this at times if he is trying to lead his man away from the scoring area or into a defensive trap. He may also over-play a man if he knows which way he prefers to go. He should be comfortable in his stance but not so comfortable that he may go to sleep. He can give more ground if the man with the ball is far from the scoring area. He must not let the offensive man fake him out, or leave his feet on a fake. He should slow down the movement of the offensive man as much as possible, sliding with the dribbler, and never crossing his feet. Try to make the offense play in an unfamiliar manner, and attempt to upset the balance of their attack whenever possible.

Guarding the logical pass receivers

The aggressive man-to-man defensive player does not wait until his man receives the ball to start playing defense. He must play full-time defense, contesting all leads and passes in to the nearest, most logical pass receivers. The man guarding the man who does not have the ball does not assume a position of a direct line between his man and the basket. He assumes a part-way position between the man and the basket, and the man and the ball. How far the defensive man shifts toward the ball will vary with the individual and the man that he is guarding. The defensive man must quickly learn how far he can safely go to cover his man well and still contest passes that may be made to him. It is difficult for a man to score a basket if he can't get his hands on the ball.

The basic defensive position is with the inside foot forward, the outside foot to the rear, and both hands extended from the sides. The knees should be flexed and the weight equally distributed between both feet. The defensive man should face ⅔ toward the man and ⅓ toward the ball, extending one hand toward the passing lane and the other hand toward the possible cutting lane. The defensive man should keep his eyes on his opponent's belt-buckle and use peripheral vision on the ball. He should not be faked out by the feet or head and shoulder moves of his man. The offensive man is not going to go anywhere that he does not take his pants.

The defensive man must be balanced and ready to move in any direction at all times. He must use his peripheral vision to watch the ball and to be alert for possible screens. The other defensive players must warn of possible picks or screens. Contest all cuts by the offense and force the offensive man to cut behind your back. Anticipate the offensive man's moves and then beat him there.

Guarding the man in the lane

A man in the lane is in a very dangerous scoring position. The best defense against him is to prevent him from receiving the ball within the lane area in the first place. The old saying, "an ounce of prevention is worth a pound of cure," is very applicable here.

In covering the men in the lane who do not have the ball we divide the lane into three areas. The first area is the low post area, which is the position of the first rebounders on the foul lane. The second area is the middle area, which is the position of the second rebounders on the foul lane. The third area is the high post area, which is the area of the third rebounder and the foul line (Diagram 12-7).

In defensing the man without the ball in the low post area, we play in front of the offensive man at all times. The defensive man assumes a side stance between the ball and the man, with his body turned so that he can watch both the ball and the man. Here the rule is the opposite of that for the man guarding the logical pass receiver—⅔ toward the ball and ⅓ toward the man. The feet are nearly parallel, the body weight equally bal-

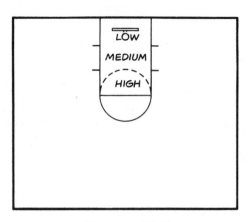

Diagram 12-7

anced, and the arms are extended. The arm toward the ball is up pointing the ball, and the other arm is extended to the side toward the low post man. The defensive man must watch the ball and also anticipate breaks by the low post man. The weak-side forward must give the low post man vocal help and may also have to help him out on a lob pass over his head. On a shot, the defensive man must move around the low post man and get good rebounding position against him.

In playing the man in the middle area the defense can either play in front of or at the side of the man. If the medium post man is covered from the side, the defense is close with one arm extended in front of the man. The feet are straddling one leg of the opponent, with the outside leg in front of the post man. The side position changes with the position of the ball on the floor. If a guard has the ball, the post man is straddled from the foul line side. As the ball is passed into a forward, the defensive man must roll in front of the post man and then assume a side position, on the baseline side of his man. He must not go behind his man in changing positions, because his team will be able to get the pass to him too easily. He should be careful to watch for the break or lob pass. Again the weak-side forward may have to give assistance to the defensive post man.

When the offensive man is in the high post area it is best to cover him from the side. The side position on defense is similar to the side position in the middle area, straddling one leg of the opponent, with one arm extended in front of the man. The defense should play a little farther from the man, in order to be

152

ready to cover a possible break or roll. In changing side positions, as the ball is moved, the defensive man should go behind the high post, instead of in front of him.

These rules for guarding the man in the lane apply not only to the normal pivot man but also to any man who moves into the lane area at any time.

Playing the weak side on defense

The weak-side defensive man turns toward the ball in a ⅔ position, with a ⅓ position on the offensive man. He should sag toward the middle of the floor and toward the ball. The distance of the sag will vary with the distance of the ball from the man. The weak-side man attempts to watch the ball, the over-all playing situation, and his man all at the same time. If the man makes a cut for the lane area or toward the ball, he must beat him there. He should over-play the man toward the ball, in order to force any pass to be a lob pass over his head.

He must make the offense take low-percentage gambles, watch the over-all play situation, warn other players of screens, picks, and other potentially dangerous situations, and give good vocal assistance. If a potentially dangerous scoring situation develops where he can stop the score, he should move in to do so, telling other players what he is doing, so they can help him out and pick up his man.

Switching on the aggressive man-to-man defense

As a rule we switch on the aggressive man-to-man defense, only when it is absolutely necessary. If a defensive player has committed an error or allowed his man to get too far away from him, he may call a switch. (If he does this too often he may be asked to rest on the bench for a while.) If a man runs into a screen, he turns and guards the screener. The man who was guarding the screener should pick up the other offensive man. This is a rule, but it is not taken for granted. The man who was screened off should call for help. The defensive man who is covering the man coming around the screen, should move out to pick up the man as quickly as possible. If the man behind the screen reverses, the switch-back must be just as aggressive.

We attempt to slide through whenever possible against the screen. The man who is defensing the screener may have to take a step back in order to let the defensive man through. Either defensive player may call the switch, but it is the responsibility of the man who is screened off to call for help whenever he thinks he is in trouble. "Take him," "I'll pick him up," "I've got him," "Switch-off," "Help," "Watch the screen," are valuable phrases to be used on defense. After a switch has been made, we attempt to switch back to the original man, at the earliest opportunity. This switch-back should be smooth and executed when there is little offensive threat in the area. It should be made with the fullest knowledge and co-operation of both defensive players who are involved.

Rules for using the aggressive man-to-man defense

1. Play the man with the ball tight man-to-man when he is in scoring position.
2. Play the logical pass receivers partway between the basket and the ball, covering both the pass and the cut.
3. Play in front of all men deep in the lane.
4. Take up a front or side position on men in the middle lane area (go in front while changing positions).
5. Take up a side position on men in the high post area (go in back in changing positions).
6. Contest all passes into the lane or good scoring positions.
7. Force the cutter to go behind your back.
8. Switch only when absolutely necessary (slide through when you can safely do so).
9. Call all switches and move out aggressively to pick up the man coming around the screen.
10. Switch back as soon as possible.
11. Don't start to play defense *after* your man has the ball.
12. Use peripheral vision on the ball and watch for screens.
13. Watch the man first and the ball second, but try to keep them both within your vision.
14. Use good defensive form and balance.
15. Watch the offensive man's belt-line and don't be faked out.
16. Do everything that you can to slow down the offense.
17. Sag on the weak side. Don't play your man too tight if the ball is a safe distance away.

18. Talk on defense. Communication is vital to good defensive play.
19. Make the transition from offense to defense as quickly as possible.
20. Anticipate plays and try to lead the offense where you want them to go rather than vice versa.
21. Study your opponent. Quickly size him up and don't make the same defensive error against him twice.
22. Remember that a man cannot score unless he has the ball. Keep the ball away from him in his favorite scoring positions.
23. Try to encourage lob passes but do not take foolish chances which will require someone else to pick up your man.
24. Force the offense to play in an unfamiliar manner and upset their balance at every opportunity.
25. Be aggressive! There is no time to rest while playing defense.

13

The Alternating
Zone Defense

The alternating zone defense is the second "A" of the Triple-A defense. It is a vital part of the total defensive plan. Many people refer to zone defense as an easy defense to teach, or as a defense that is not as tiring nor demanding as man-to-man. They claim that the players can get more rest on defense and therefore are better prepared for offense. We are not inclined to agree with their theorizing. There are advantages to using a zone defense, but we do not include these points in the list.

First of all, any defense is hard work—for the coach and the players. I do not know of any easy way or short cuts for teaching sound defensive fundamentals. A player must have good individual fundamentals—balance, poise, proper footwork, timing, quickness, alertness, positioning, use of arms and hands, knowledge, and desire—to be able to play any kind of defense.

Second, if a player rests on the zone defense, he is not doing his job properly. The zone defense must constantly be on the move, changing positions with each pass. If one player is weak or rests the other four men must carry the load and cover for him. The zone defense requires more teamwork than the man-to-man. If every man does not do his job properly the total defense is in danger of collapse.

The alternating zone defense idea

The alternating zone defense is a method which is devised to surprise and confuse the opponent. Just about when the offense thinks they have the defense figured out, you are in position to make a change to confuse them. Each time you change your defense, the offense must be prepared to make adjustments to counteract your strategy. If the offense is not prepared to play against all defensive styles they are in trouble. If they are prepared, they are bound to be stronger or weaker against certain styles. It is up to the defense to challenge them, find out their weaknesses, and employ the defense which is most effective.

Even though the offense may be prepared to change their strategy against a new defense, a change is likely to cause disorganization and confusion for a while. This short period of offensive confusion may be the turning point in the ball game. It may cause the offensive team to lose their momentum, to become discouraged with their patterns, and to lose their confidence in each other. This is all a part of the psychology of the versatile basketball team.

The defense must be sure that they are creating the confusion and are not a part of it. The defense must be well prepared. They must know what they are trying to do and when. Every player must be in on all changes of defense and prepared to make them effectively. The alternating zone defensive team must understand all of the basic zone principles and be prepared to apply them from several different floor positions. The alternating zone defense must be able to stop any man-to-man attack and be able to change to meet any zone attack.

Advantages of the zone defense

The zone defense is very widely used in basketball today and therefore must possess certain advantages. First, and not the least among them, is the element of surprise. Some teams are very well prepared against a man-to-man defense but freeze up when they are confronted with the zone defense. The fact that you have more than one defensive style gives the other team more to worry about.

The zone defense can be very effective in stopping the screening offense. It eliminates the need for switching and therefore cuts down on defensive confusion resulting from the weaving offense. The zone can be very difficult to penetrate in the middle, either by a drive or by inside passes. The zone defense is a team defense and very difficult for an unorganized offense to confront. Two- and three-man plays can be readily stopped by a concentrated five-man defense. The free-lance style of play is not too effective against a zone.

With the use of this defense the best rebounders can be kept in good rebounding position near the goal. The quicker defensive men can be kept in good out-court position. This puts the zone defense in an ideal position from which to start the fast-break attack.

Some of the assets of the zone defense are summarized as follows:

1. It stops the screening offense.
2. It stops the driving-and-cutting offense.
3. The defense is strong in the middle.
4. It prevents inside passes and cuts.
5. It concentrates the defense on the dangerous man—the man with the ball.
6. It stops two- and three-man plays.
7. It stops free-lance offenses.
8. It can be used with other defenses to surprise the opponent who is not prepared.
9. It can keep your best rebounders in good inside position.
10. It can keep ball hawks or quick men out court.
11. It gives a good position from which to start the fast break.

Some disadvantages of the zone defense

The zone defense is a team affair. If one man fails to shift or to do his job properly it will weaken the total defense. Each man must be fast and well organized to stop the fast break. Placing one man in a given area of the floor allows the opponent to overload the defense by putting more than one offensive man in an area covered by only one defensive man. The zone defense is usually weak against a good out-court shooting team and in the corners of the floor. The zone defense must shift rapidly and in unison to adjust to each pass which is made. The zone defense may have difficulty when the team is behind in score and the opponent resorts to a ball-control game. Many teams that rely on the zone as their major defense have not really fully developed the man-to-man defense. They are therefore usually weak in trying to use the pressing-type game. Their attempts to play in this unfamiliar style usually results in disaster.

Some of the liabilities of the zone defense are summarized in the following list.

1. It requires the utmost in teamwork.
2. It may be weak against the good fast-breaking team.
3. It is susceptible to overloading by the offense.
4. It may be weak against good out-court shooters.
5. It may be weak in the corners and in shifting from one side of the floor to the other quickly.
6. It cannot be used effectively when you are behind in the score late in the game or in overtime.
7. Man-to-man fundamentals may not be developed properly if you rely too much on the zone defense.
8. The zone may keep good rebounders on the inside, but does not always give a one-on-one situation in blocking out for the rebound.

Basic principles of the zone defense

Many of the basic fundamental principles of man-to-man defense are incorporated into the zone defense. If a player does not have good defensive fundamentals it will be difficult for him to play any type of defense effectively.

A zone defensive player must be able to play the man with the ball on a one-on-one situation. The chief difference is that he has plenty of help behind him in doing so. He must be able to stop the dribbler, pick up a man on the drive, slide from one position to another, use the arm and hands effectively, use good footwork, block out on the rebound, use peripheral vision, anticipate moves, protect the passing lanes, and be able to use many other basic defensive fundamentals well.

The basic idea of the zone defense is just the opposite of the man-to-man. The man-to-man defense plays the *man* first and the ball second. The zone defense plays the *ball* first and the man second. This variation in concentration by the defense is the chief difference between the two defenses.

The zone defensive players watch the ball and must shift their defensive position each time that the ball is moved. The zone players are responsible for certain areas on the floor. They do not venture too far from these areas, but there must be an overlapping of all areas. When the opponents move from one area to another they are checked off to men in the new area. The zone defense is usually two or three men deep between the ball and the basket at all times. The men in the zone must be ready to cover the ball at all times. If the other team puts two men in one area or if one defensive man cannot shift properly, other players must be ready to move in and help cover for them. The zone requires more co-operation and teamwork than any other defensive style.

The various phases of the alternating zone defense

The alternating zone defense has three basic zone defensive phases: the two-one-two phase, the one-three-one phase, and the one-two-two zone phase. These three phases are developed and co-ordinated into a basic defensive unit. These units may be alternated at will in various game situations.

Later in the season certain combination defenses may be developed and added to the alternating plan. These are the four-man zone—one man-man-to-man and the three-man zone—two man-man-to-man defenses. These combination defenses may be used to confuse the opponent in certain game situations. If a team has one or two stars one of these combination defenses may be most effective in stopping them. Most coaches would much rather face a team with a star than a balanced five-man offense any day of the week. This should be an important point to keep in mind in developing your team offense.

The two-one-two defensive phase

The basic floor arrangement on the two-one-two zone phase is with the two smallest and fastest men out court, the tallest man at the foul line, and the other two players (good rebounders) in the inside positions (Diagram 13-1).

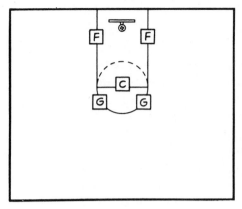

Diagram 13-1

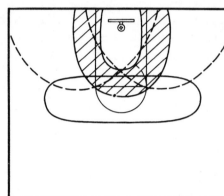

Diagram 13-2

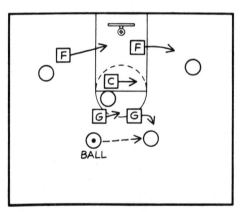

Diagram 13-3

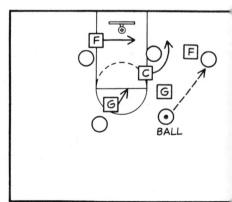

Diagram 13-4

Basically, the two guards cover the area from about three feet inside the foul line to a step or so outside the middle of the foul circle (shown by the solid lines in Diagram 13-2). The center man plays the foul-line area, always between the ball and the basket, from the foul line to the base line (shown by the diagonal lines in Diagram 13-2). The two forwards cover the deep areas under the goal and on the sides of the floor (shown by the dotted lines in Diagram 13-2). All of the areas overlap each other and players may leave their assigned areas if it becomes necessary for them to do so in order to cover the man with the ball.

This defense remains tight in the middle. The outside men do not chase the ball too far out front or too deep on the sides. There should be a man covering the middle area (between the ball and the basket) at all times. There should be at least one man underneath the goal area at all times. This defense should be two or three men deep between the ball and the goal at all times. See Diagrams 13-3 and 13-4 for the various shifting assignments.

The center is the key man on this defense. He must not only cover the center area, but he must also be ready to move out to cover the ball in the corners or high on the side if he is needed (the back forwards normally cover the corners and sides). He must be the quarter back, and talk up the defense and call changes of areas if necessary. If the center is forced to leave his area the man that he is covering for must sag quickly into the middle. The weak-side men are also ready to help out if they are needed. Each time the ball is passed, the defense must shift toward the ball.

Use of the two-one-two zone defensive phase

The two-one-two phase is very strong in the middle but may be a little weak outside or in the corners. It may be used to stop a team with a good inside scoring threat, particularly from the high post position. This defense may have trouble with a good one-three-one offensive attack or a good out-court and corner shooting team. It may be used as a surprise element for short periods against them, but can not usually be employed for too long against this type of team. The two-one-two defense gives good rebounding position and is ideal for starting the fast-break attack. The three inside men can form the rebound triangle. The two outside men can play the high bounding ball and be in good position to break out to receive the quick pass out, and to go with the fast break.

The one-three-one defensive phase

The floor positions of the one-three-one defensive phase are with a point man (P), two wing men (W), a center (C), and one man under the basket area (L). The point man would be the fastest ball hawk on the squad. The wing men should be quick and able to move well. The center area may be covered by the big man and the under basket area may be covered by a lanky, agile player who is a good rebounder (Diagram 13-5).

The basic areas covered by each man are shown in Diagram 13-5. The point man covers the area around the foul circle, although he may cover the wing position if the wing man goes to the corner (shown with the solid line in Diagram 13-6). The center covers approximately the same area that he covers on the two-one-two zone, the high post area from the foul line to the base line (shown with diagonal lines in Diagram 13-6). The low post man covers the base line and under the basket. He shares the corner responsibility with the wing men (shown with the dotted line in Diagram 13-6). The wing men cover the sides and may go to the corner if no man is at their wing spot. If the low post man goes to the corner, then the weak-side wing may have to cover the under-basket area (shown with arrows in Diagram 13-6).

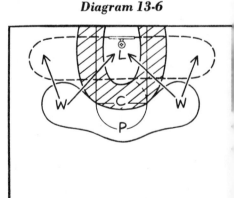

Diagram 13-6

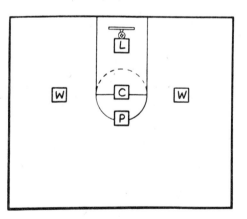

Diagram 13-5

This phase of the alternating zone defense should be three men deep between the ball and the basket at all times. There should be one man on the ball, one man in the center area, and one man back under the basket no matter where the ball is located. Two men should be in position to contest passes and the movement of the ball at each side of the middle man.

Use of the one-three-one zone defensive phase

The one-three-one zone defense phase is strong up the middle but may tend to be a little weak on the sides, particularly out front and in the corners. This phase is very effective in stopping the middle man, men near the foul line, or a man driving for the goal.

The change to the one-three-one defensive phase forces the offense to alter their normal offense zone attack. If they are using a one-three-one attack against the two-one-two phase, the change into the one-three-one may make their offense bog down. This phase may also be very effective against a one-two-two or a three-two attack by the offense. The one-three-one may be strong on the inside against a two-one-two attack but may have difficulty around the circle area on the outside.

The one-three-one phase does not give as ideal a rebounding position as the two-one-two. The weak-side wing man must move in on the board with the shot. The rebound triangle is formed by the low post man, the high post, and the weak-side wing man. The man covering the ball must be ready to play the high bounding rebound with the point man and head for the fast-break position. This defense does not complement the normal fast-break pattern as well as the two-one-two. Each player must think and move, as soon as the ball is shot, into the proper rebounding and fast-break position. Many teams have difficulty coping with the one-three-one zone defense. It is one of the hardest zones to penetrate.

The one-two-two zone defensive phase

The third phase of the alternating zone defense is the one-two-two. This defense has one man on the ball at all times, two backing him up (playing the men and also the passing lanes), and two men covering the under-basket area. This puts four men between the ball and the basket at all times. The outside point man

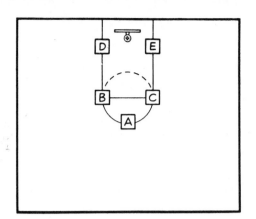

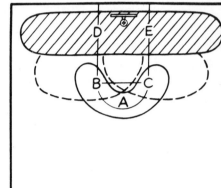

Diagram 13-7

Diagram 13-8

(A) should be the quickest man on the squad, and it is also help-ful if he has long arms. He should try to cover the ball as often as possible on the outside. The next two men are his back up men (B and C). They must cover the area behind the point man against drives and passes into this area. Players B and C should be agile and able to shift quickly to cover the passing lanes. The farthest men back under the goal, D and E, should be the best rebounders on the squad (Diagram 13-7).

Diagram 13-8 shows the basic floor area covered by the various players with the one-two-two zone. The point man attempts to cover the man with the ball near the foul circle area, out court as much as possible (solid line). If the ball is passed to the side, B or C has to move out to cover the man with the ball (shown with dotted lines). If he does move out, then the point man breaks into his place on defense. Players D and E cover the under-basket area, but may have to move out in the corner to cover a man with the ball. If D or E moves out, then B or C must break into the position vacated near the goal. This defense attempts to maintain the one-two-two alignment at all times as the ball is moved from one area to another, covering the inside areas very tightly.

166

Use of the one-two-two zone defensive phase

The one-two-two zone defensive phase is a very hard defense to penetrate or to get good inside shots against. This can be a very aggressive, hard-working type of zone defense, particularly against the inside men. It gives opportunities for double-team situations on the inside as men split responsibility on the various players. This defense may be a little weak in the corners and on the shift from the weak side.

This defensive phase may be very effective against a team which has several tall inside players and attempts to utilize the low post offense. It can force the taller men to come outside in order to receive passes. The big men are usually not nearly as effective on the outside.

The one-two-two zone may have difficulty against the one-three-one offense, which puts a man on the foul line and a man on each side of the foul line on the outside. In this situation two men are forced to split the coverage against three men on the inside. In this situation you may want to move up one of the under-basket men to help if the situation becomes too difficult to cover from the regular one-two-two assignments.

Alternating the zone defenses

The various phases of the alternating zone defense can be changed by several different methods. They may be designed to be changed by the coach, the game situations, the offensive pattern of the opponent, or by a defensive captain. The different phases may be given code names or numbers.

In the first method the coach may give a signal to the defensive captain as he falls back on defense. The team will use that defensive phase until a new signal is given. If one particular phase proves to be effective, it may be employed until the coach feels that a change may be necessary.

With the second and third methods the game itself may call the defensive style. You may use one phase after a scored field goal, another after a free throw, and so on. You may want to use definite defensive phases against certain offensive alignments. Some teams like to match up their zone defenses with the type of zone offense which is employed against them.

One man on the team should be designated as the defensive

captain. You may at times want to give him authority to set up or change defenses during the game. He should be responsible for seeing to it that all players know what you are trying to do on defense. The other team members must learn to look to him each time that they come back down the floor on defense. He must be a very responsible leader who is capable of thinking while on the basketball court.

Give him responsibility but keep the major decisions with the coaching staff. Do not force him to be responsible for possible failures of strategy. The coach should have broad shoulders and be able to bear any failures which may occur in connection with basketball strategy.

Switching assignments with the alternating zone defense

Hold to a minimum the changes in areas which must be made by individual players in changing from one phase to another. One player may become an out-court specialist on all defensive phases, another man may play the middle area on all zone phases, a third player may be an under-basket specialist. This means that only one or two players must make major adjustments from one phase to another.

In changing from the two-one-two phase to the one-two-two only one man must make a major change. One out-court guard must drop back into the circle area, and the other foul area man is bumped over (Diagram 13-9).

In switching from the one-two-two to the one-three-one only one major change is required. One of the under-basket men moves up to the foul line at the side. The man who played the middle area on the two-one-two also plays the middle on the one-three-one. The middle position on the one-two-two is played much in the same manner as it is with the one-three-one. This makes it easier for players to become proficient in playing a given area, and defensive confusion is held to an absolute minimum (Diagram 13-10).

In changing from the one-three-one to the two-one-two, the wing man who normally plays under the goal on the one-two-two drops back under. The middle man stays in the middle area and the other wing man comes out front with the point man (Diagram 13-11).

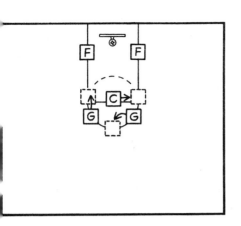

Diagram 13-9

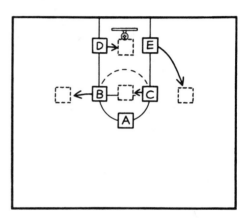

Diagram 13-10

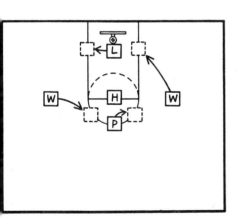

Diagram 13-11

Develop each phase of the defense independently

You can see that it is possible to play three different phases of zone defense with very little change in floor areas on the part of the individual players. You may develop a point man as an out-court zone specialist, a man as a foul-line area defensive specialist and an under-the-basket defensive authority. Only the two wing men must learn to play in more than one area. One of them can be an out-court middle man and the other wing man can be a middle under-basket player.

This style of alternating zone defense is not as complicated nor as hard to teach as it may seem at first glance. Once the players get the idea of all three zone phases they learn to alternate areas very quickly. The various phases can be taught as individual defensive units and then welded together into one basic defensive unit. If you attempt to throw the whole defensive idea at them at once, they may become confused. Develop each phase as the players are ready to learn. In the end you will have a sound, well-developed, versatile defense which is prepared for any situation which may develop.

14

The Aggravating
Press Defense

The third "A" of the Triple-A de-
fense is the aggravating press. The aggravating press can become
just that to the team that is not fully prepared to face *all* aspects
of this versatile defensive attack. This defense is designed to
cause confusion, discouragement, and disorganization among the
opposing players. Some coaches contend that a basketball team
can only learn to play one type of defense with any degree of
skill. This old idea is about to pass the way of the old ideas concerning the two-hand set shot. The game of basketball has
evolved greatly since the days of the center jump and is still
changing.

The modern game of basketball requires more individual offensive and defensive skills than ever before in its history. A player
can no longer get by playing only one phase of the game. Just as
the jump shot has revolutionized the offensive game, the versatile
defense is now in the process of revolutionizing modern basketball. More and more teams are using the press defense and are

using it with more skill and in many new and different game situations. The gambling aspects of the press defense are being minimized by increasing knowledge and skills. The idea of the press defense is changing from that of a rebel defense to more of a science.

The psychology of the press defense

Psychology is a very important part of the art of coaching. Nowhere is it more important than in the application of the press on defense. Each team member must be fully convinced of the soundness of the basic team defense. He must have confidence in his own defensive ability. He must also feel assured that he has the backing and support of each of the other members of the squad. The press defense must exhibit the utmost in confidence. This confidence will not only assure each defensive player but will also be an important factor in causing the offense to become demoralized and disorganized. A press defense which is lacking in confidence will also be lacking in effectiveness.

Confidence is built through knowledge and experience. Some coaches hold the press for emergency situations only, such as when they are behind in the score late in the game. Too often the lack of actual experience shows during these situations. If the press has been used in other games where it was not just an emergency, the team is better prepared to execute it effectively when it is really needed.

The basic principles of the aggravating press defense

The aggravating press defense does not attempt to steal the ball on every play. The aggravating press attempts to force the offense into making mistakes. The idea is to disrupt the continuity of the offense. Aggravate them, then wait for opportunities to come along. Be prepared to seize all opportunities and to capitalize on all fundamental errors. The aggravating press causes opportunities, it doesn't wait for them. We try to force the other team to beat themselves.

Our philosophy of the press is, "If you can't help us, don't hurt us." We attempt to instill the proper balance of daring and caution. We tell our players that if they can use the press and not give up the snow-bird or lay-up shot, we are not hurt. We do not expect a player to steal the ball each time, nor do we expect him to allow his man or area to get easy shots. If the press does not work, it has only cost a little energy to try.

The idea of the aggravating press is to get the ball back again as quickly and cheaply as possible—that is, without fouling or giving up the high percentage shot at the goal. If you do not get hurt on the press and make it work even one time in ten or fifteen tries, it is worthwhile. As a rule any gambling should take place when the defensive man has plenty of help behind him and not when the loss of the gamble would result in an easy scoring opportunity.

The full court man-to-man press phase

The man-to-man phase of the aggravating press has each player picking up a man in a given area of the court and then playing him man-to-man. One guard takes the man throwing the ball in bounds and the other guard takes the first logical pass receiver. Each forward picks up a man on his side of the floor. The pivot man covers the mid-court area and is responsible for the offensive man farthest down court. The players do not play a particular player, they simply pick a man in their area and are then responsible for him man-to-man after that time (Diagram 14-1).

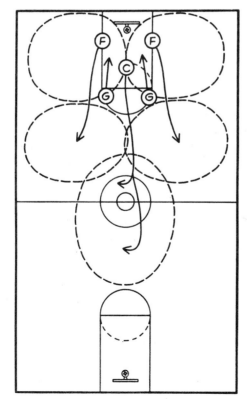

Diagram 14-1

The man who is playing the man who is taking the ball out may either play him tight or else fake and drop back to help cover the throw-in of the ball. On the man-to-man defense each player takes a position between the ball and his man until the offense is able to get the ball across the center line of the court. The idea is to contest passes in the back-court area. The defense should try to force the opponent to make passes over their heads and then be ready to pick off or knock down the passes.

Players may have to switch to cover the man with the ball if he gets away from his man. The dribbler must be stopped. The side lines may be helpful in slowing him down or stopping this threat. When a dribbler is stopped he is covered very closely to force quick or careless passes. Two-time situations are not encouraged but may be taken advantage of in the back-court area, where a player could still hustle back if his man breaks up court.

The full-court zone press phase

The basic setup of the full-court zone phase is a two-two-one zone. It is similar to the man-to-man setup as far as the floor positions are concerned. The difference is of course in the execution. The similarity in floor positions makes it difficult for the offense to know which phase you are going to use at any given time.

The two-two-one zone defense will not cover the man who is throwing the ball in bounds. It will allow the first pass to be made in to positions at the middle or side of the floor, where it will be easy to make double-team situations on the ball. The man to whose man the ball is first passed must stop that man when he starts his dribble and try to force him to make a reverse turn. As the turn is made the nearest man must move over for the double-team situation. As the double-team is made the men in the other two nearest areas must cover the logical pass receivers and also the passing lanes. The man in the farthest area from the ball covers the back man and watches for the long pass.

Applying the two-two-one court press

The basketball court is divided into five general areas. The foul line and an imaginary line up the center of the floor serve as dividing lines. Player 1 is assigned the lower-left area, 2 the lower-right area, 3 the middle-left, 4 the middle-right and 5 the middle and back area (Diagram 14-2).

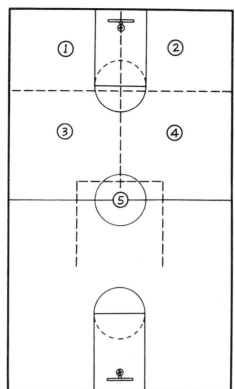

Diagram 14-2

Each player will pick up the man in his area. If there is no man in his area, that player will sag to the middle of the floor. Players 3, 4, and 5 will play between the man in their area and the ball. Players 1 and 2 will play their men on the inside and will not contest the pass into the very low area of the floor (the lower six or eight feet near the base line). Long or careless passes are encouraged by playing between the man and the ball in the back areas. The defensive players should not drift too far toward the ball side. They must be ready to beat their man wherever he is going in his area. They must look for pass interceptions or deflections, but they must be able to get back fast if the other team is successful in getting the ball over his head.

Alignment against the pass into the low area on the two-two-one

If the ball is passed in low, the man in that area waits for the man to start his dribble and then overplays the dribbler to the outside. This will force the dribbler into a position where the double-

175

team can be applied. Player 2 will break over for the double-team, preferably after 1 had stopped the dribbler and forced him into a reverse turn. Player 2 must make sure that the dribbler is stopped and does not get up the middle away from 1. When the double-team is applied, 3 and 4 must cover the men in their areas and in the passing lanes. Player 5 must try to help cover the center circle area if possible, but must be responsible for the man farthest down the court.

If the dribbler after being stopped is successful in passing the ball up court to an open man in 3's or 4's area, 3 or 4 must cover the man who receives the pass and stop his dribble, trying to force a reverse turn. If the ball was passed into area 3, 3 will cover the man with the ball. Player 1 will break over for the double-team situation. Player 4 will break across the floor to cover men and passing lanes behind the ball on the side. Player 2 will break back into the area which was vacated by 4 and pick up any men in this area. He will also look for careless passes and attempt to prevent movement of the ball up this area. Player 5 must try to back up 4 and 2 in their new areas and also protect against the long pass (Diagram 14-3).

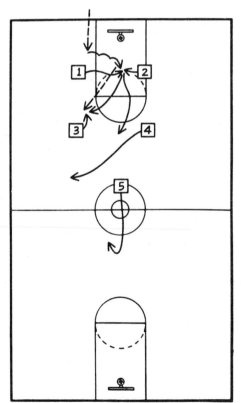

Diagram 14-3

Anytime the ball passes a defensive player he must run for his life to get back into defensive position. A player should never trot down the floor side by side with his man if the ball is ahead of him. The two-two-one defensive alignment must be maintained at all times. If and when the offensive team is successful in getting the ball across the center line, the defense must retreat and get organized into whatever regular defense they are using at the moment. It is of the utmost importance to be well-organized on defense as soon as the offense is in scoring position. The press idea may be dropped and the regular zone or man-to-man defense employed as the opponent crosses the center line. In some situations you may want to continue with the two-two-one press principles in order to go get the ball when necessary.

Alignment against the pass into the middle area on the two-two-one

If the throw in bounds is made into the high side or middle area, 3 or 4 must cover the throw in. If the ball is passed high on the side 4 will cover the man with the ball. Player 2 will come up for the double-team and 3 and 1 will cover the backup areas. Players 3 and 1 will cover both men and passing lanes and 5 will back them up and cover against the long pass (Diagram 14-4).

If the ball is then passed right back to the man coming on the floor after the throw in, 1 must stop his dribble and force him toward 2. Player 2 will come back for the double-team. Player 3 will break back to cover the middle of the floor area, while 4 breaks back to cover the area formerly covered by 3. Player 5 still maintains the back-court area. Any time that the ball passes a defensive player he must run full-steam to get back and help out the team defensive effort.

The half-court zone press phase

The half-court zone press phase is basically a one-three-one aggressive zone defense which has been extended out to the mid-court area. The half-court press can be used as a surprise weapon out of the regular one-three-one zone defense from time to time. This defense is also very effective in going out to get the ball if it becomes necessary. It gives the opportunity to double-team the man with the ball out-court against a team that is trying to hold on to the ball.

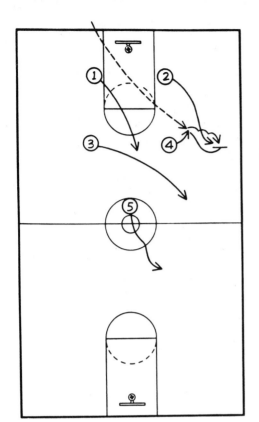

Diagram 14-4

Diagram 14-5

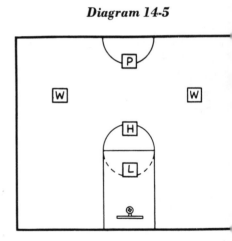

The basic setup is with the point man (P) near the edge of the center circle. The wing men (W) are at each side of the floor, about halfway between the foul circle and the center circle and about eight feet from the side lines. The high post (H) defensive man is out near the outer edge of the foul circle. The low post (L) defensive man is in the foul lane behind H, about four feet from the foul line. The same men should play the extended areas of the one-three-one zone defense who play these positions on the regular one-three-one zone defensive phase (*see* Chapter 13). The basic defensive setup is shown in Diagram 14-5.

Applying the half-court press

The half-court press can be in position and waiting as the offense brings the ball up the court, or they may fall back into the one-three-one zone and then break up into the half-court press when the offense nears the center line of the floor. This may be a good surprise move from time to time.

The point man must be the aggressive man as the ball is brought across the center line. He waits until the defense attempts to dribble the ball across the line and then charges out and over-plays his man to the inside attempting to drive him into a favorable double-team situation with a wing man. The wing man will charge up to stop the dribbler and try to force a reverse turn. If the dribbler does get through the middle, he is going into the strength of the zone. The wing man must not make his move too soon on the double-team. As soon as the wing man does move to double-team, then the other wing man must sag toward the middle and the middle high post must move to cover the area vacated by the wing man on the strong side. The weak-side wing man and the high post man must then play both men in their own areas and in the passing lanes. The low post defensive man must back them up and cover the under-basket area. On double-team situations the zone really becomes a two-two-one alignment (Diagram 14-6).

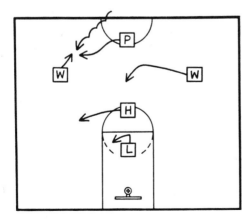

Diagram 14-6

The weak-side wing man (W-2), and the high post man (H), must be prepared to prevent inside passes and also be alert for interceptions or pass deflections on rushed or careless passes. If the offense does get a pass into the middle area the weak-side wing man (W-2) must pick up the man with the ball. The high post man must break back to the middle and out to the W-2 wing position if necessary. The point man (P) must quickly leave the double-team and take the high middle area of the zone. W-1 stays on the right wing position. The low post man still covers the lane area. W-2 will over-play the dribbler and try to force another double-team situation with W-1 on the right or with H, who is now playing the left wing position.

If the ball is passed into a deep corner the low post man (L) must move out to cover the ball. When he moves out the high post man (H) must rush into the lane area to assume the low post man's area. The weak-side wing man must sag into the middle. The point man (P) sags into the foul circle, and the strong-side wing man can play the side and be alert for a possible double-team opportunity if the low post man can force a dribble toward his position.

Shifting positions on the half-court press

The half-court press requires the utmost in hustle, teamwork, and individual thinking. Gambles must be reduced to well-calculated risks. Slow reactions or the failure of any man to move into his proper area after each pass could result in very dangerous situations. The zone must always be maintained basically as an aggressive one-three-one zone defense, shifting into a two-two-one only when favorable double-team situations present themselves. If the two-two-one double-team does not produce results, the zone must shift immediately back into the one-three-one alignment on the very next pass.

The three-quarter-court zone press phase

The three-quarter-court zone press defense phase is basically the half-court press, extended from the center circle to the backcourt foul circle. The zone principles of the half-court press also apply to the three-quarter. Once you learn the half-court press, you can very easily have a second press, with which to surprise the opponent. This is the beauty of having a pressing defense which can be used as a half-court defense or else be extended into a larger area. The three-quarter press will give more pressing time as the offense comes up the court. The ten-second psychology is helpful with the three-quarter defense. Many times if one defense is not effective a quick switch into another phase may be very disconcerting to the opponent. These are all good reasons for having a versatile defense.

The basic alignment on the three-quarter press is with the point man (P) in the middle of the back-court foul circle, the wing men (W) on each side of the court, halfway between the center line and the foul circle and about eight feet from the side line, the middle high post man (H) at the outer edge of the center circle, and the back defensive man or the low post man (L) behind the center circle (Diagram 14-7).

Diagram 14-7

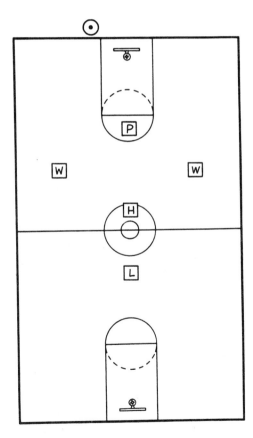

Applying the three-quarter press phase

The three-quarter press allows the ball to be passed in bounds, below the foul line, without contesting the pass. When the man with the ball starts to dribble up court, all defensive men will contest passes and cover men in their areas. The point man will over-play the dribbler and try to force him into a double-teaming situation, with one of the wing men. If a double-teaming situation occurs, the weak-side wing man and the high middle area men will cover behind the double-team to prevent passes to men up court. The back defensive man (L) will cover the area behind them against the long pass.

If a pass is successful the man into whose area the ball was passed must stop the movement of the ball. The men who were in on the double-team must hustle back to get into proper defensive position in front of the ball. The low post man should be alert for pass interceptions, and any time that he is out of position the high post man must be ready to break into his area to cover for him.

Using the aggravating press defense

The aggravating press defense can be a very demoralizing defense when it is executed properly. The press can be used as a full-time defense, a sometimes defense, a surprise defense, or an emergency defense. You must have the proper personnel and some depth on the bench in order to use it as a full-time defense. With most personnel it can be used as a sometimes defense or a surprise weapon. If you use the press only as an emergency measure, it will not be too efficient, but it could pull one out of the fire for you. The press must be used in practice and in actual game experience if it is to be a polished, aggressive, confident part of your total defense.

Some teams like to spot-press on signal or by key during the game. They may press on odd or even scores, after a scored foul shot, etc. This is often a disrupting influence against the poised offense. The type of press can also be varied on signal or key. The aggressive press can be changed from a full-court man-to-man back into a half-court press. The half-court can then be extended into the three-quarter press. The full-court man-to-man press can be switched into a full-court zone press, or vice versa. It will be very hard for the offense to figure out if you are using the full-court zone or man-to-man defense. This is one advantage of having a zone defense which assumes identical floor positions as the man-to-man. A team that does not have at least one press defense ready to go is not really prepared to play modern basketball.

15

The Kaskaskia Red-Dog
Double-Team Press

The Red-Dog double-team press
has been a very effective defensive weapon used by basketball
squads at Centralia Junior College (now known as Kaskaskia
College). Our players love to play aggressively, and this defense
gives them a lot of opportunity to use all the skills that they
possess. This style of play gives the players a feeling of accom-
plishment when they are victors, and if they should suffer defeat
they have some feeling of satisfaction, a feeling that they put forth
every possible effort to bring home the victory.

This defense has contributed greatly to the many scoring rec-
ords which our teams have made in past seasons. This aggressive
defensive style used with an effective controlled fast-break pattern and a perpetual pattern of offense, has produced a prolific
scoring machine and has been responsible for many of our victories. We sometimes use this defense for long periods of time.
We may use it in emergency situations late in the game or even
early if we trail by too large a margin. This aggressive defensive

style has helped our squads turn many "certain defeats" into victories.

The Red-Dog idea

The Red-Dog defensive idea is a go-and-get-'em defense. It applies pressure on the offense on a full-time basis. The Red-Dog never gives up. This defense starts to dog the offense the minute they regain possession of the ball in any manner. The Red-Dog does not take time to rest or let up. The defensive players must be in better physical condition than the opponent—and they must prove it. This defense is not just a full-court or a half-court press, it is a continuous full-time press. If the double-team situation does not work out on the first attempt, than the defense must quickly fall back, regroup themselves, and try again and again.

The Red-Dog takes chances but knows when and how to take them. This defense attempts to make up for some of the inherent weaknesses of a pressing style of play through knowledge, skill, and plenty of hustle. We have used the Red-Dog defense successfully against some of the best junior college basketball teams in the country. Many of these teams were well drilled against most presses, but they often weakened under this constant pressure.

Principles of the Red-Dog double-team press defense

The Red-Dog double-team press defense utilizes both the man-to-man and the zone defensive principles. It begins as a non-assigned man-to-man defense, with each defensive player picking up a man within a given area. Pressure is always applied on the ball, and possible double-team situations are encouraged. As soon as the first double-team situation presents itself, the defense switches into a two-two-one zone defense on the ball. If the double-team does not produce the desired results, the defense falls back into the aggressive nonassigned man-to-man defense with the first successful pass. New double-team situations are sought and the defense is ready to crash back into the two-two-one zone as soon as a second man goes for the man with the ball.

The Red-Dog press defense does not concede anything to the offense but makes them earn anything that they get. The marriage of the zone and man-to-man principles makes this defense able to accomplish many things that neither of these defenses could do by themselves. The quick setup of the man-to-man prevents the easy throw in bounds, and the zone principles can be most helpful in containing dribblers or ball-handlers who would be very difficult to stop on a strictly man-to-man basis. The zone principles can also make the screen a very ineffective offensive maneuver. The man-to-man phase can counteract moves to over-load or over-shift the defense. The zone principles can help to give good floor balance and put men in favorable position in order to cash in on lob passes, telegraphed passes, long throws, wrong reverse turns, and other errors.

The combination of zone and man-to-man defensive principles makes it very difficult for the offense to decide upon a method of attack against the Red-Dog. This hesitation as to which offensive attack to use may be the "pause that refreshes" for the defense. If the offense starts spending too much of their energies and concen-tration in trying to figure out the defense, they may neglect offensive concentration. This can produce enough tension and confusion to make the defense just that much more effective. A couple of thoughtless errors by one or two men can cause a chain reaction which may completely unnerve and upset the offense. Many well-drilled and composed teams seem to fall into this pattern.

How to use the Red-Dog double-team press

The first setup on the Red-Dog is an aggressive man-to-man defense. All in-bounds passes are contested and the opponent who gets each rebound is quickly pressed. Each player is responsible for picking up a man in a given area as soon as the transition from offense to defense occurs. On a scored goal or free throw one guard will be assigned to cover the man throwing the ball in bounds and the other guard will cover the first logical pass receiver. The forwards will pick up the next two closest men on each side of the floor. The pivot man will rush to the middle of the floor and will be responsible for covering the offensive man farthest down the court. Each player quickly takes a defensive position between his man and the ball. The idea is to force passes over the head of the defense and to watch for careless passes (Diagram 15-1).

If the pass in bounds is successful, then the man who is covering the man with the ball will over-play his man to one side or the other and attempt to lead the ball into favorable double-

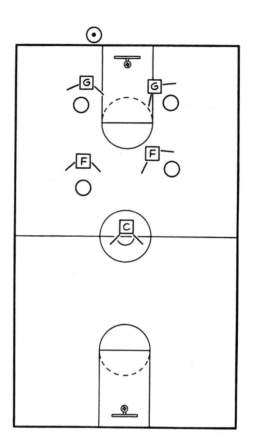

Diagram 15-1

teaming situations or to stop the dribbler. The man coming out on the double-team must have proper timing, and he must move aggressively and with the arms extended to prevent quick passes when he makes his move toward the ball.

Changing from man-to-man to zone

As soon as the second man commits himself to the ball, then the rest of the team must change their defensive strategy. The defense must quickly change from an aggressive man-to-man into a two-two-one zone defense. Every player on the team must be involved in the transition. The change must be quick and efficient. The strategy is to rush the ball and attempt to excite the passer into a wild or careless pass. The back three defensive men must cover the other four players. They must take halfway positions and anticipate passes and movement of men within the zone.

Reversing the defense from zone to man-to-man

If a successful pass is made from the double-team situation, these two men must quickly fall back and each defensive man must pick up an offensive player. The aggressive man-to-man is now in effect. The man who is covering the ball will again over-play his man and attempt to create new double-teaming situations. This alternating man-to-man zone press will continue all over the court on a full-time basis. The Red-Dog will continue to apply pressure on the ball as long as the other team maintains possession on either end of the court.

The Red-Dog alignment after a rebound

After a rebound the closest man to the rebounder must cover the rebounder and slow down the first pass out, in order to allow the other defensive players to get into their proper defensive areas. The alignment after a rebound is the reverse of the normal Red-Dog, with the three inside players (the center and two for-

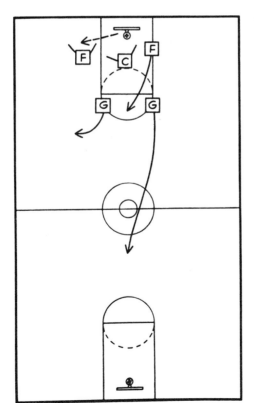

Diagram 15-2

wards) applying the pressure on the ball. The guards fall back and cover the two farthest players who are going back on offense. If the center covers the rebounder, the two forwards will be responsible for the two men closest to the ball and the guards must pick up the men breaking down court. If a forward is pressing the rebounder, the center and the other forward must quickly cover the two players nearest the ball. Each player will play one man using the aggressive man-to-man principles. The movement of the ball must be stopped. If a pass up court is successful, the bypassed players must break down court into better defensive positions. The quick transition from offense to defense is of utmost importance in applying the Red-Dog press after a rebound (Diagram 15-2).

Reorganization of the Red-Dog

After each defensive player has picked up a man and the defense is set, the overplay principle and the double-team situations may be anticipated. If a double-team play occurs, then the man-to-man principles are switched quickly into the two-two-one zone defense. On each successful pass the defense must quickly fall back into the man-to-man, with the pressers dropping back to cover open men.

The most essential ingredients in any press are hustle and organization: without these the Red-Dog cannot possibly be a success. After the opponent has crossed the center line, the defensive players look for favorable times to switch men, in order to have a well-matched alignment. After the matchup occurs and the defense is in a more favorable rebound and man-to-man position, the overplay can be applied out court and double-team situations can be sought out court or in corners. When this occurs, the two-two-one zone principles may be applied in the half-court situation. In playing the dribbler, the inside hand should be used on the ball and the man should be over-played. The defense does not wait for the offense to make the action, they attempt to create the action and to lead players where they want to go.

When to use the Red-Dog defense

The Red-Dog is an excellent have-to defense. It is a very good defense to use in order to attempt to pull out a victory from some very unfavorable situations. It may be used when you are behind in the score late in the game. It is a very good weapon to use against the stalling team that is trying to maintain possession of the ball. This defense does not sit and watch the seconds tick off the clock, it does something about regaining possession of the ball.

The Red-Dog may be used as an effective weapon at any time against a team that has a definite height advantage over your squad. If the short team drops back and waits for the big man to put the ball up against the boards, they may never see the ball again until it passes through the net. Some teams may be forced to remove their big, slow men and insert smaller, quicker players to combat this style of defense.

The Red-Dog may also be used as a spot or shocker defense. It may be applied from time to time during the game in order to surprise and confuse the opponent. This application may be on a signal from the bench, from the defensive captain, or at a pre-arranged game situation. The system that is used must be easily recognized by each player.

This defense, as with all defenses, must be well practiced in order to be of any true value when it is really needed. Practice time must be allotted for defense. Actual game experience is also essential in order to develop the Red-Dog to the ultimate degree of preparedness for emergency situations.

Some assets and liabilities of the Red-Dog

The Red-Dog is a very useful defensive weapon to have in your arsenal. Some of its advantages are summarized as follows:

1. It derives positive values of the man-to-man defense.
2. It utilizes the positive values of the zone defense.
3. It applies pressure on the ball at all times.
4. It forces the offense to play in an unfamiliar manner.
5. It creates team spirit.
6. It may tire and demoralize the opponent.
7. It allows double-teaming of the ball.
8. It stops the dribble effectively.
9. It forces quick or careless passing.
10. It is a very hard defense to attack.
11. It does not allow a team to hold or stall the ball.

12. It creates desired offensive action.
13. It gives the defense security and hope in unfavorable situations.
14. It is useful in combatting taller or slower teams.
15. It can be used to "shock" the offense.
16. It gives players an opportunity to fully develop defensive skills.
17. It requires players to think on their feet.
18. It derives full value from a physically well-conditioned team.
19. It combines principles which are used in several defenses, and it is consistent with other defensive styles which are employed (Chapters 11, 12, 13, and 14).
20. After the development of the man-to-man press and the zone press, it is very easy to assemble and teach.

Some of the disadvantages or liabilities of the red-dog defense are summarized as follows:

1. It requires depth and bench strength to be used for long periods.
2. Like all press defenses it requires much organization, knowledge, skill, and hustle to operate effectively.
3. It requires top physical and mental conditioning.
4. It cannot be fully developed until late in the year or after the basic defenses and presses are learned.
5. Like most presses it may have some elements of gamble.
6. It may be more effectively employed by some personnel than by others.
7. It requires good defensive ability and fundamentals.

16

Adapting the System
to the Players

Some coaches know how they are
going to play basketball from one year to the next. They have
a set style which they employ and they play the same way each
year. Their players must fit the mold and be able to adjust to the
system. This is fine for teams that can pick and choose their
player personnel to fit the system which they employ. Unfortunately most small college and high school coaches are not this
fortunate; they must learn to utilize the material which they have
available. How well the player material is utilized and developed
is the measure of their success.

The coach who must do the best he can with the material that
he has at hand must learn to be flexible and resourceful. He must
be willing to start from scratch each year and build from the
ground upward. He must be open-minded concerning offensive
and defensive strategy. He may have to tear up last year's plans
and completely draw up new ideas for his new type of player
material. Trying to fit square pegs into round holes can become

quite a problem. The easiest and best solution may be to find out first what kind of pegs you have, before you attempt to match them to the holes.

Know your players

Many coaches spend hours scouting the opposition but don't really know their own team members. Time spent early in the season in testing, observing, and analyzing your player material may save much grief and many hours of work later in the season. Early-season plans should be somewhat flexible, and time should be taken to correct errors at the time that they occur. Plans must be developed for building an effective offense and defense for the kind of material which is available. The coach may have to change his thinking several times, and he may have to do some experimentation and careful analyzation before coming to any definite conclusions.

The coach should ask himself many questions concerning his personnel: How would I defense my team? Where are our weak links? What individual weakness could the opponent exploit? What strengths do we seem to have? How about team moral and spirit? How many one-way players do we have? What do the prospects for improvement seem to be? How quick do the players seem to grasp new ideas? The answers to these questions and many others could give an indication as to the steps necessary to develop a winning team.

Testing your players

Unfortunately no one has as yet developed a good basketball ability indicator. There is no one good test or device which can pick your players or tell accurately the degree of their skill and knowledge. Much of this is left up to the individual judgment of the coach. The coach must base as much of his judgment on facts as possible. There are several good tests which may be employed to aid the coach in the formation of his opinion and judgment of player personnel. These tests are not infallible but they do give a good indication of individual and team strengths and weaknesses.

Speed tests

We like to check the speed of our players over measured distances early in pre-season practice. We use the 50-yard dash, the

100-yard dash, and 220-yard dash to get some idea of their speed. We do not usually give these tests until after a conditioning and training program has been initiated. This gives the players time to become physically conditioned and they are not as apt to pull muscles or sustain other injuries early in the year.

Half-court elimination races may be run. Three lines may be formed at one end of the court and the loser in each race will be eliminated. The first two finishers go to the end of the lines and go again. When you have eliminated all players except one, you may have challenge races to determine the fastest players in the half-court dash.

Quickness tests

Speed on the basketball court is not always for very long distances. Sometimes quickness is just as important as sustained

Diagram 16-1

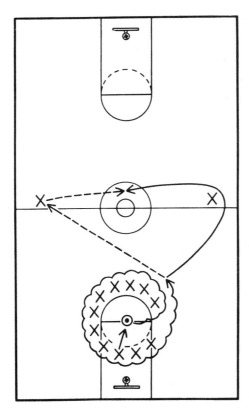

speed. Quickness tests may be devised to measure reaction on the basketball court.

One simple test that we use to check ability to react quickly is the circle-call drill. In this drill all but two of the players gather around the free-throw circle at one end. One player is placed near the side line on each side of the floor near the center line. The ball is placed in the center on the foul line. When the coach calls a player's name, he must grab the ball off the floor, dribble out the opening at the foul line, dribble around the outside of the foul circle once, pass the ball up to the player on the left side, cut around the opposite outside man, and meet a return pass at the jump circle in the center of the floor. Individual times may be recorded (Diagram 16-1).

Wall-bounce test

The wall-bounce test is a combination passing and quickness test. Each player stands behind a line about 8 feet from a wall. Upon a signal from the coach, he passes the ball against the wall, so that it rebounds back into his hands. The coach times the player or group of players for one minute. The number of passes made in that time is recorded. Players must stay behind the line during the test.

Cross-over lay-up test

The cross-over lay-up test is a combination jumping, shooting, timing, and quick reaction test. A player is given a ball under the goal and must shoot a lay-up shot on the right-hand side of the goal, grab the ball out of the net, and shoot a lay-up on the left-hand side of the goal. He alternates from right to left and back again. The coach times each player for one minute and the number of goals scored is recorded.

Jump-reach test

The distance that a player actually can jump from the floor may be recorded by the jump-reach test. A player stands next to a wall and stretches one arm upward as high as he can reach. He makes a mark on the wall with a piece of chalk at that point. He then jumps as high as he can and makes a mark with the chalk at that point. The distance from the first mark to the second is the jump-reach distance. This is the actual distance that the player is getting his feet off the floor. Three attempts may be made and the best distance recorded.

Ball-tip test

Another simple jumping and timing test is the ball-tip test. A player throws the ball against the backboard and jumps up to tip the ball back against the board. He tips it back as quickly as possible again and again. The number of times the ball strikes the board within one minute is recorded.

Physical condition and strength tests

In order to check the general physical condition and strength of the individual, one-minute tests can be given with such activities as push-ups, chin-ups, sit-ups, knee-squats, and jumping-jacks. Each activity is demonstrated and it must be performed in the prescribed manner or the score is not recorded.

Endurance tests

Basketball as it is performed today is a very rugged sport and requires much in the way of endurance. Some teams are front-runners who look very good during the first half or three-quarters of play, but fall apart late in the game. Much of this is due to poor physical conditioning. Good conditioning, both physical and mental, is vital to winning basketball games. The early season conditioning program should be well planned and the team must not be allowed to grow stale during the long season.

Endurance tests or checks should be used early in the pre-season practice and from time to time during the year. One test that we use is the long-distance run. If we are able to use the outdoor track, we time our players in the one- and two-mile runs. If the weather does not permit, we set up an indoor course equal to these distances. The time of each individual is compared to that of previous runs which have been recorded. We hope to see a constant improvement in performance. If times start to drop, we seek possible causes of this change.

Some of the previously mentioned one-minute tests may be used for endurance also by removing the time limitation or increasing it to two minutes. For example you may see how many chin-ups, push-ups, jumping-jacks, or sit-ups that a player can perform in order to get an indication of his general physical endurance.

Shooting tests

Shooting ability may be checked by counting the number of buckets made in a given number of shots from the free-throw line or from various marked spots on the floor. A basketball "golf course" may be laid out for this purpose.

The ability to shoot under pressure or in game-like situations may be checked by laying out a prescribed course on the floor and seeing how long it takes a player to go around it, scoring at each spot. Numbers are placed on the floor with adhesive tape. The player must shoot the ball from each spot until he scores the basket. He must retrieve his own rebounds and return to the given spot to shoot each time. A stop watch is used to check the time that it takes each man to go completely around the prescribed course. Players may compete with each other and one man may be used on defense to attempt to distract the shooter. The defensive man cannot block the shot or interfere with the shooter other than by fakes, feints, waving arms, or talking to him.

Interpretation of tests and data

Data from the basketball and physical ability tests should be recorded for each player on a large chart. The coach may study and interpret the results of all of the data. Individual performances may be compared and charted. The tall pivot players may be compared with each other. The smaller guards may be compared with each other. The performances of this year's squad may be checked with the results from previous years' performances.

A general over-all comparison may be made by giving points to each player in each event. The results are divided into four parts. The best one-fourth performances in each event may be given 4 points, the next one-fourth 3 points, the third one-fourth 2 points, and the bottom one-fourth given 1 point. The individual points earned in each event may be totaled and compared with the point total of other individuals. For example, if a player was in the top ¼ in 50-yard dash he would receive 4 points; the top ¼ in the 100-yard dash, 4 points; the second ¼ in the 220-yard dash, 3 points; the top ¼ in the half-court dash, 4 points; the top ¼ in the circle-call test, 4 points; and the third ¼ in the wall-bounce, 2 points; he would receive a point total of $4 + 4 + 3 + 4 + 4 + 2 = 21$ points. Each player's total score may be charted and compared with the others'.

The results of these performances may also be grouped according to categories, such as all speed tests in one group, all quickness tests in another, etc. The same form of scoring and comparison may be used here. It may also be desirable to chart and compare individuals according to their positions on the team, stressing or passing over qualities which are more or less essential for each position. This type of comparison may actually be of more value than the straight comparison mentioned above.

Developing the offense around the material

After a careful analysis of the abilities of individual players from test data and general observations of fundamental drills, ideas should be formed concerning the style of play which may be employed most effectively by the squad. Basic floor alignments may be chosen to put players into positions which would use their assets to full advantage. For example, if you have a small, quick squad you may want to employ a spread-type of offense. This will help to pull the defense out away from the basket and allow the players to use their quickness to take advantage of tight play. The rebounders will also be pulled out and your quick, smaller men can move in around the defense for the rebounds. If you have a big, slow player, you may want to keep him on an inside position at all times on the offense, in order to take advantage of his size. If you have slow guards, you may want to keep them out court as much as possible, so that they will have a head start in getting back on defense. If your guards and forwards are about equal in ball-handling and rebound ability, you may want to rotate them during the offensive pattern.

Special plays may be developed to take advantage of special offensive abilities. Some players may have spots or definite shots on which they score most effectively. Plays or patterns may be built around these strengths. Last year's plays may have been very effective for last year's material, but they may not be the best plays for this year's squad. Certain plays on general patterns may be stressed and other options may be used sparingly or dropped altogether.

Fitting the defense to the material

The general effectiveness of a style of defense depends not as much on the type of defense as upon how it is executed. Just as with the offense, the defense should be patterned to fit the players. The coach in addition to his many other skills, must be a good tailor. A store-bought suit may look pretty nice, but a tailor-made suit is more desirable. A store-bought offense or defense may fit pretty well, but a little tailoring can go a long way in making it much more effective.

A big, slow squad may just as well forget the press defense, except as a surprise or emergency weapon. They may, however, be able to develop a very effective zone defense. They may even be able to develop a good half-court press by utilizing one or two quick players out court. The small, quick squad may be forced to press for long periods of time to use their skills to best advantage. On defense as with offense you may want to limit the movement of certain players in order to use their individual skills to full advantage. Combination defenses may be built and developed around the abilities of the individuals.

Developing reserve strength

Every basketball player on the team hopes to be on the starting five. Many coaches choose the starting five and then forget the rest of the squad. They spend most of their time and energy with the first team, with a resulting neglect of the development of reserve strength. It is very hard for a reserve to sit on the bench during the game, be ignored in practice, and still grow and develop as a basketball player.

On the other hand, the coach must have his best players on the floor most of the time if he is to produce a winning squad. Only five players are allowed on the floor at one time and the coach must spend most of his time with the boys who show the most promise. Indiscriminate use of reserves in a ball game can cause play to become disorganized and ragged. The answer to this problem is not an easy one. If a coach uses his reserves only in emergency situations, they are not usually ready to be of much help to the team. Without reserve strength, the team is not likely to go very far in tournament play. The coach must do his best to win each game, but he must also have an eye on the future. The success of the basketball season will depend upon how well the squad is prepared to face any given situation at the end of the year.

Keeping these things in mind, the ideal situation is to have a squad which has depth. It is best to have at least seven or eight players of equal strength and use them. If you have only five players who are definitely superior to the rest of the squad, you must use them in order to have a winning team, but you must concentrate on the development of at least two reserves. These reserves must be used at every opportunity and must fit into the play of the starting squad.

The idea of a starting seven

We like to have a starting seven—that is, to develop a starting line-up which can be altered to best meet the opposition. We feel that we must have at least three guards who can play the two guard spots and not slow down the effectiveness of the squad. We feel that we need at least four men who can play the three inside positions. The starting combination of these seven men may be varied to produce the desired results. A certain combination may give you the best size and rebounding combination, another may give you needed speed, and yet another may be best for certain offensive patterns, etc.

This seven-man idea can make your team much more versatile. It can maintain continuity in offense and defense and prevent excited play in emergencies. The loss of one or two players by way of fouls or injury is not as apt to interfere with the play of the team as a whole. With a seven-man starting unit you are better prepared for the long journey of tournament play. This idea of play is a help to the reserve problem, but the pitfall of neglecting other players in practice and in games must still be avoided. If you have only five players that you feel must be starters, then you must still attempt to develop the seven-man idea at every opportunity in practice and to substitute these men as often as it is possible to do so in games.

Basketballology

The modern game of basketball is a science. Scientific attitudes and methods are essential for success. Since the development of the jump shot, the fast break, the controlled fast break, press defenses, combination defenses, match-up defenses, the shuffle, revolving offenses, etc., basketball is better and more complicated than ever before. There is no comparison between basketball as it was played in the 1920's, 30's, or 40's and basketball of today. The modern player has much more skill and knowledge and is more versatile. The players of today are taller and stronger physically than before. Today's basketball team cannot get very far unless they have versatility and knowledge of many basketball styles. The modern coach must be a successful teacher, psychologist, sociologist, and good scientist.

Do you have problems?

Coaching is not an easy occupation. Each coach has unique problems and situations which he must face every day. Things that work well for one coach may not be successful for another. Things that work well one year may not succeed the next. Some coaches have good physical facilities and coaching aids while others have poor facilities and equipment. There are scheduling difficulties, conflicts with other social and school activities, school bus problems, injuries, illness, personality conflicts, and public relations problems. Practice time is often a problem. How do you teach everything with so little time? These are just a few of the many problems of coaching.

Where does basketball fit into the entire school program? What are the values of basketball for the individual player? The student body? The community? What am I accomplishing? These are all questions that the coach must ask himself. A good philosophy for the troubled coach may be found in this old prayer: "God grant me the serenity to accept those things which I cannot change, the courage to change those things which I can change, and the wisdom to know the difference."

Index

203